Fabulicious!

Fabulicious!

TERESA'S ITALIAN FAMILY COOKBOOK

from author of the *New York Times* bestseller,
Skinny Italian

TERESA GIUDICE

With Heather Maclean

RUNNING PRESS
PHILADELPHIA · LONDON

Published by Running Press,
A Member of the Perseus Books Group

Books published by Running Press are available at special discounts for bulk
purchases in the United States by corporations, institutions, and other organizations.
For more information, please contact the Special Markets Department at
the Perseus Books Group, 2300 Chestnut Street, Suite 200, Philadelphia, PA 19103,
or call (800) 810-4145, ext. 5000, or e-mail special.markets@perseusbooks.com.

ISBN 978-0-7624-4239-3
Library of Congress Control Number: 2011923388

E-Book ISBN 978-0-7624-4309-3

9 8 7 6 5 4 3 2
Digit on the right indicates the number of this printing

Cover and interior design by Frances J Soo Ping Chow
Photographs provided by Teresa Giudice: pp 12-13, 25, 72, 98,
125, 132, 145, 146 (top right, courtesy of Andrew Coppa),
155 (bottom left, courtesy of Neil Abbey), 176, 181, and 186
Edited by Jennifer Kasius
Typography: Affair, Archer, Baskerville, La Portentia,
Neutra, Sweet Rosie, and Swingdancer

Running Press Book Publishers
2300 Chestnut Street
Philadelphia, PA 19103–4371

Visit us on the web!
www.runningpress.com

DEDICATION

To my adopted family: my friends and fans from around the world. You inspire me every day with your fabulousness! Your support and kindness mean the world to me.

To my own fabulicious family: my amazing husband Joe and my girls Gia, Gabriella, Milania, and Audriana. Every day when I wake up and look at you, you make me so happy. Thank you for letting mommy be a working mom now. I love you, I love you, I love you.

To my amazing in-laws Filomena and Franco Giudice and the entire Giudice family. I have been lucky enough to know you since I was born, you welcomed me into your family, and have always supported and loved me. Thank you. I love you!

And for my mother and father. You've always added love to everything you do in and outside the kitchen. Thank you for raising me and Joey in a house of love. Ti amo più delle parole.

ACKNOWLEDGMENTS

 huge thank you to the amazing people who helped make this book a reality. Thank you for your tireless efforts, vision, and support! I could not have done it without you!

Susan Ginsburg, the most fabulous agent anyone could ever have—you are brilliant and wonderful!; the entire staff at Writers House, the best agency in the world!; the incredibly talented group at Running Press, especially Jennifer Kasius, Nicole DeJackmo, Chris Navratil, Craig Herman, and Frances Soo Ping Chow; culinary god Rick Rodgers; photographer Ben Fink and his team; and a very special thank you to my amazing writer and friend Heather Maclean.

Contents

Chapter 4

Bread from Heaven

Chapter 5

The Lighter Side of Life

Chapter 6

Antipasto: Come On-A My House

Chapter 7

The Main (Meaty) Event

Chapter 8

The Wild Side

Chapter 9

Food Fit for a Feast, a Party, or a Potluck

Chapter 10

Last (Minute) Suppers

Chapter 11

A Happy Ending

La Famiglia

Ciao, Bello!

I can't help it. Every time I sit down to write this intro to my *Italian Family Cookbook*, two things keep popping into my head: that cheesy Olive Garden commercial, "When you're here, you're family"; and what I said about Caroline Manzo when she insulted my meatballs on the *Rachael Ray* show: "Caroline's as Italian as the Olive Garden."

If you read *Skinny Italian*, you know I'm not a huge fan of Olive Garden because it takes traditional healthy Italian dishes and turns them into heart-clogging servings of ungodly proportions. (Forget *Jersey Shore,* it's the Olive Garden that gives us Italians a bad name!) I am, however, a huge fan of Caroline Manzo. (Even if she's only ¹⁄₁₆ Italian, or whatever she is . . .)

Caroline is the older sister of my youngest daughter's godmother. Get it? I know with big Italian families it gets complicated real quick. My baby Audriana is the goddaughter of Caroline's baby sister Dina Manzo. And Jacqueline Laurita, who is married to Caroline and Dina's brother Chris Laurita, is one of my best friends. But while everyone on *The Real Housewives of New Jersey* seems to be related, I am not related to any of the Manzos or Lauritas (or, thank you sweet baby Jesus, the Staub/Merrills.) By blood, anyway. By heart, we're all family.

> *When in Rome . . .*
> Famiglia = fah-MEAL-ya

My mama and papà with my girls and brother Joe's family.

Joe with his siblings, Peter and Maria.

That's how it is with us Italians. Family is the cornerstone of Italian life. Our entire social structure, our economy, our politics, and, of course, our food is centered around family. We spoil our kids rotten, so much so that they never want to leave home. Albie and Christopher Manzo are adorable, but don't let them fool you. Their "L" in "GTL" (Gym-Tanning-Laundry) is "Leave it for Mom." That's just

Me with another famous Italian mom, Caroline Manzo.

how it is, and how we moms like it. I lived with my parents until I moved in with my husband (that's how good Catholic girls where I come from do it). My mama and papà still come over to my house almost every day (and no, contrary to Internet rumors, they do not live with me, and they do not live in my basement—my house doesn't even have a basement!). I see my brother, Joe Gorga, his wife Melissa, my niece Antonia, and nephews Gino and Joey several times a week. Same with all of Joe's sisters and brothers, their families, my cousins, my aunts, and my mother- and father-in-law . . . and no, we don't always get along. Do I sometimes wish my cousin would stop with the lame jokes? Yes. Do I wish my baby sister-in-law didn't copy everything I do down to the shoes I wear and the chairs on my front porch? Of course! But you know what they say: "You can't pick your family."

Well, half of them anyway. You can't help where you were born, but you can go out and make your own family. To me, family is everything—not just the family I came from, but also the family I made. I think it's the most important thing we ever do in life—to find and build our own family. And to me, "family" is not just the people you are related to, it's the people you love. Your spouse, sure, and your children, but also your partner, your best friend, your dorm mates, your sorority sisters, your friends at church . . . they're all your family.

I get letters all the time from people telling me they wish they were Italian or they wish they were part of my family. Let's clear this up right now: YOU ARE! Italians count their close friends as family. And you, sweetheart, are as good as gold. I wish I could have every one of you to dinner at my house, but for now, let me bring my kitchen to yours.

So welcome to my Family Cookbook! Salute!

Tanti Baci,
Teresa

Oh, and that Meatball Throwdown on *Rachael Ray*? I want a rematch! I thought we were cooking *authentic* Italian food. Caroline deep-fried her meatballs. Deep-fried? Who does that? Does she serve fried Twinkies for dessert? You could deep-fry a sock and it would taste better than a baked meatball . . . although I guess you might not live long enough to enjoy it!

There I go smack talking again. Buckle up, Baby Dolls. This is not your mama's cookbook.

CHAPTER 1

We Do It My Way

If you bought my first, unbelievably successful *New York Times* best-selling cookbook, *Skinny Italian*, *grazie, grazie, grazie* from the bottom of my heart. If you didn't, there are a few things you missed that are crucial to cooking my way (which, of course, is the right way). Since you'll need them for this book, here are the Cliffs Notes, or Spark Notes, or whatever they call cheating in school by not reading the actual book these days . . . .

My Name Is . . . My Name Is . . .

Let's get this out of the way right away. I know you've heard it pronounced "Jew-dice," but the correct way to say my last name is like this (quickly, and with an Italian accent please): Judy Chay. Get it right. Tell your friends. (Thank you. Thank you very much!)

Olive Oil: The Only Oil

In *Skinny Italian*, I dedicated an entire chapter to this healthy liquid gold (Chapter 3: Blessed Virgin Olive Oil). I told you to use it every single day. It's a little more expensive than vegetable oil, yes, but what you'll save in medical bills later will more than make up for it. I try to never, ever, ever use vegetable oil. Not even

> *When in Rome . . .*
> ## Giudice = Jew-DEE-chay

when I'm baking. And you'll see in this entire book, there is not *one recipe* that calls for vegetable oil of any kind, including that crazy canola oil.

Of course, there are tons of different kinds of olive oil, and in my last book, I told you how to shop for it, store it, and serve it. Here's the take-away: only use EXTRA-VIRGIN OLIVE OIL. Period. Nothing else matters. If you can, look for a bottle with olives picked and pressed in Italy, but the most important thing is the EXTRA-VIRGIN part.

SPICE GIRL

To be a great cook, you have to know a few basic things about how to cook with herbs. For the most part, use FRESH basil, garlic, parsley, rosemary, and thyme. Use DRIED oregano and sage. Most herbs can go into your cooking at any time, but you should add basil and parsley toward the end.

Garbage In, Garbage Out

It goes without saying that the better quality ingredients you use, the better your final dish will be. Fresh Parmigiano-Reggiano cheese cooks and tastes better than plain Parmesan, but it's also harder to find and a bit more expensive. Get the best your budget can afford. If you want to substitute Parmesan, feel free. Your recipes will still rock, I promise. Just promise me you won't buy anything powdered in a non-refrigerated can.

Finger Cookin' Good

When I'm in the kitchen, I have my hands in everything. And I mean everything. Part of enjoying your food is touching it, caressing it, working it good with your hands. I do a lot of mixing with my hands. I knead with my hands. You can use fancy mixers and kitchen tools, but to me, the best cooking involves just you and the food. (You know I'm all about "cleansiness" so of course I always have clean hands when I cook.)

✳ ✳ ✳ Teresa's Tip ✳ ✳ ✳

It might seem like a shortcut to just use canned *chopped* tomatoes, but it's not a good one. They add chemicals to the can to keep the pieces looking perfect (kind of like the fast-food burgers that never, ever decompose . . .). We don't like unnecessary chemicals, especially when cooking for our family, and we want the pieces to melt, not just sit there and look pretty. (Come on, tomatoes—you're not too pretty to work!)

Please Squeeze the Tomatoes

One of the cornerstones of Italian cooking is a good red sauce. And you can't get a good red sauce without breaking up the tomatoes because you need the smaller pieces to melt into the sauce. If you're not using fresh, use *whole* canned tomatoes (imported Italian plum tomatoes are best). Hold the can over your pan, reach in carefully, and squish the tomatoes into chunks as they slide out through your fingers. You want the pieces to be the size of large stuffed olives. And go ahead and pour the juices from the can in there as well.

FABULICIOUS IS AS FABULICIOUS DOES

As so many of you have written me and attested—I already knew this because I have four kids and don't work out—if you eat home-cooked, fresh, authentic Italian food, you can have your pasta and your skinny jeans, too. It's a natural diet with lots of fresh veggies, fish, light sauces, and our friend, olive oil. But since this book is a family cookbook, and growing kids shouldn't be on a calorie- or fat-restricted diet (and since I have a "no obsessing about your food" rule), I'm not including the complete nutritional information in this book. I try to cook as healthfully as possible, but not all of the recipes I'm giving you are meant for weight loss; some are once-in-awhile, let-loose celebration dishes.

But don't worry, more than half of the recipes here are, in fact, "skinny." I have marked them with this pretty icon: ⓢ. And whenever I can, I give you substitutions to make a recipe "skinny," so look for the ⓢ sidebars, too!

And since so many of us are multi-tasking, working maniacs, in addition to giving you a whole chapter of quick-and-easy meals, I've also marked all "quick" recipes that can be on the table in 30 minutes or less with this icon: ⓠ.

✳ ✳ ✳ Substitute This ✳ ✳ ✳

Most of my recipes include the full-bodied flavors of things like heavy whipping cream and fresh mozzarella cheese. I have no problem cooking with these things because they're used in such small quantities that what you get per serving isn't a big deal. And a lot of time, with reduced-fat products, you're just trading in fat for extra salt (lots and lots of extra salt). So read the labels! But if you want to, you can always substitute light cream for heavy cream, and reduced-fat cheese for regular cheese. But I will not allow you to substitute margarine for butter (no way, no how) or *anything* for extra-virgin olive oil. No sir!

SAUCE-TACULAR

With a good base sauce, you can make a million variations. I gave you one—The Quickie Tomato Sauce—in *Skinny Italian*, and since it's so yummy and used so many times in this book, I'm gonna give it to you again. I'm also giving you a new base sauce that's a little hotter. The Quickie is a sweet sauce; Snappy Red Sauce is spicier. Feel free to interchange them in any of the recipes to match your mood. If you want to add more basil or oregano to either one, be my guest, but keep in mind that those flavorings are usually in the finished dish, too, so you could unintentionally reach herb overload.

The Quickie Tomato Sauce

Makes about 3½ cups, enough for 1 pound of pasta

1 tablespoon extra-virgin olive oil

1 (28-ounce) can imported whole Italian plum tomatoes, broken up with their juices

¼ cup tomato paste

2 tablespoons chopped fresh basil

1. Heat the oil in a large saucepan over medium heat. Add the tomatoes and their juices and the tomato paste. Bring just to a boil.

2. Reduce the heat to medium-low and add the basil. Simmer to blend the flavors, about 10 minutes. The End.

Snappy Red Sauce

Makes about 3½ cups, enough for 1 pound of pasta

1 tablespoon extra-virgin olive oil

1 small onion, chopped

¼ teaspoon salt

2 garlic cloves, minced

½ teaspoon red pepper flakes

1 (28-ounce) can crushed tomatoes in thick purée

3 tablespoons chopped fresh Italian parsley

1. Heat the oil in a large saucepan over medium heat. Add the onion and salt. (A little salt brings out the onion flavor.) Cook, stirring occasionally, until the onion is translucent, about 5 minutes. Add the garlic and red pepper flakes and stir until the garlic is fragrant, about 1 minute.

2. Stir in the tomatoes with their purée and the parsley and bring to a boil. Reduce the heat to medium-low. Cook at a brisk simmer, stirring occasionally, until slightly reduced, about 5 minutes. Serve hot as a pasta sauce.

Audriana's Pesto

✦ ✦ ✦ ✦ ○ ✦ ✦ ✦ ✦

Makes 1 cup, enough for 2 pounds of pasta

Pesto is another go-to sauce that I use for hot dishes, cold dishes, pasta, sandwiches, you name it. So here is my best recipe, named for my sweetest younger daughter.

⅓ cup pine nuts

1½ cups packed fresh basil leaves, well rinsed and dried in a salad spinner

3 garlic cloves, crushed under a knife and peeled

⅔ cup extra-virgin olive oil

½ cup (2 ounces) freshly grated Parmigiano-Reggiano cheese

¼ teaspoon salt

⅛ teaspoon freshly ground black pepper

1. Heat a small skillet over medium heat. Add the pine nuts and cook, stirring often, until lightly toasted, 2 to 3 minutes. Transfer the pine nuts to a plate and cool completely.

2. To make the pesto by hand: Using a pestle, crush a handful of the basil leaves in a large mortar (at least 2-cup capacity), pushing down with the pestle and moving your wrist in a circular motion to squeeze and crush, but not pound, the leaves. Keep adding basil leaves until they have all been crushed. Add the garlic and crush it into the mixture. Gradually work in about half of the oil. Now add the pine nuts, and crush them in. Finally, work in the cheese, then the remaining oil. Season with salt and pepper.

3. To make the pesto in a food processor: Fit the processor with the metal chopping blade. With the machine running, drop the garlic through the feed tube to mince the garlic. Add the pine nuts and pulse until finely chopped. Add the basil and pulse until finely chopped. Add the cheese and pulse to combine. With the machine running, gradually pour in the oil. Season with the salt and pepper.

4. Transfer the pesto to a small, covered container. Pour a small amount of oil over the surface of the pesto to seal it. Cover and refrigerate for up to 1 month. Stir well before using.

✳ ✳ ✳ Papà, Can You Hear Me? ✳ ✳ ✳

My father's name is Giacinto Gorga. And yes, Gia is named after him. I call him "Papà" or "Daddy," but never "Dad." He hates "Dad." To his Italian ears, it sounds like "Dead." "Don't call me Dead," he says. "I no dead yet!"

FIRE-ROASTED FROM SCRATCH

There's one more thing I want to teach you now so you can use it over and over in this cookbook (and in life): how to roast your own peppers at home. Roasted peppers, laced with garlic and soaked in olive oil, are a great secret ingredient to have in the fridge. They will last for a couple of weeks, and are perfect for putting in sandwiches and salads, laying on pizza and focaccia and just about everything except chocolate cake and cannoli. They are easy to make in the broiler, or if you prefer, you can blacken the skins on your outdoor grill.

Papà's Roasted Peppers

Makes 6 to 8 servings

7 red bell peppers
2 tablespoons extra-virgin olive oil
1 garlic clove, chopped
Salt

1. Position the broiler rack about 8 inches from the source of heat and preheat the broiler.

2. Line a large, rimmed baking sheet with aluminum foil. Place the peppers on the baking sheet. Broil, turning occasionally, until the skin is blackened and blistered all over, about 12 minutes. Take care that you just char the first layer of the thick pepper skin, and don't burn a hole into the pepper.

3. Transfer the peppers to a large bowl. Cover with aluminum foil. Let stand for 30 minutes. (The trapped steam will loosen the skin and make it easier to remove.)

4. One at a time, peel away the blackened skin from each pepper. Tear or cut the peppers into thick strips and discard the seeds. Transfer the pepper strips to a colander to let any excess juices drain, about 15 minutes.

5. Transfer the drained pepper strips to a bowl or a covered container. Drizzle with the oil, sprinkle with the garlic, and season with salt. Toss gently. Serve immediately. (The peppers can be stored, covered and refrigerated, for up to 2 weeks. The oil will congeal when chilled, so let the peppers stand at room temperature for about 10 minutes to soften the oil before serving.)

When in Rome . . .
Giacinto = Gia-CHEEN-toh

CHAPTER 2

Growing Up Giudice

Every morning when I wake up, I realize I'm not just me; I'm something much, much better: I'm a mom. (I usually realize this because there's a tiny elbow in my eye socket or a little knee poking me in the ear.) All I've ever wanted, the most important thing in the world to me, is to have my own family. With Joe and my four girls, I've been blessed beyond my wildest dreams. As every parent—and really good kid—knows, family is everything.

Having four kids under the age of nine keeps me young, fit, and constantly laughing. When I'm not running after them, I'm driving them to gymnastics, karate, birthday parties, or to see their grandparents. When I'm not singing "Ring Around the Rosie" in Italian to make Audriana dance, I'm belting out the Black Eyed Peas with Gia and Gabriella. Everyone helps everyone. The other day when we were stuck in traffic driving back from the shore, Audriana was tired and started crying. I asked Gia to play some music for her baby sister on her iPod. Three minutes later, Audriana was sleeping thanks to the Lady Gaga lullaby "Bad Romance." I live for little moments like that.

THE KITCHEN CLASSROOM

My kids want to be with me all day, every day—the day you have your first baby is the last day you ever have privacy, right? And since I cook every meal for our family, they end up spending a lot of the day in the kitchen with me. It's not just where we bond, it's also their first classroom. It's not only where they learn about how to

Schooled by Miss Milania?

✶ ✶ ✶ ✶

"Counting to 10 in Italian is so easy my baby sister can do it! Here's how you can do it too…"

1 = uno (EW-no)
2 = due (DEW-ay)
3 = tre (TRAY)
4 = quattro (KWAT-tro)
5 = cinque (CHEEN-kway)
6 = sei (SAY)
7 = sette (SAY-tay)
8 = otto (OUGHT-toe)
9 = nove (NO-vay)
10 = dieci (DEE-ay-chee)

take care of their family, but also about budgets, money, measurements, healthy eating, even reading and math.

I make Gabriella practice reading aloud in the kitchen—either she reads recipes or the ingredient boxes or sometimes she just brings a book to the counter, climbs up, and reads a chapter to the rest of us. For Gia, the kitchen is all about fractions and decimals. I have her add up the measuring cups and spoons—$3/4$ cup + $3/4$ cup equals what?—and give her money problems, like how much change would she get back if I sent her to the store with $10 and she bought $4.98 worth of stuff. With Milania, we prep for kindergarten: we cut things in halves and quarters, talk about what's bigger and smaller, and tell sequence and prediction stories: "Which goes in the pot first, the water or the pasta? What do you think would happen if I put the pasta in first?" Our favorite game, though, is "Will it float or sink?" She can spend an hour dunking things in a cup of water: macaroni, lemon seeds, pennies, my lip gloss! Even baby Audriana gets schooled in the kitchen. I count out things on her high chair tray in English, and then again in Italian.

No Such Thing As Too Many Cooks

I love, love, love to cook with my kids, but of course, they all have different jobs based on their ages. Gia, who is nine years old, is allowed to use the stove if I'm standing nearby and she's not cooking anything that might splatter and burn her. Her favorite thing in the world to cook is scrambled eggs all by herself. She's so proud when she can serve her daddy fluffy eggs on a Saturday morning.

We're also big pancake fans. After I make them (I let Gia do the flipping), Gabriella loves to take metal cookie cutters and cut out shapes for Audriana and Milania. Although hearts and flowers are her favorite shapes, we also have these great alphabet cookie cutters to teach the girls their letters. When she's done designing for her sisters, Gabriella piles the pancake scraps into a heap for Daddy, covers it with syrup, and calls it "Volcano Pancake."

There's no such thing as too many kid cooks in my kitchen (sisters-in-law, that's another story . . .). If I didn't allow my kids in the kitchen when I cooked, I'd never see them! Of course, when you're cooking with kids, you definitely have to be prepared for the entire process to be a little slower and a lot messier. One of the ways to offset the extra time those extra pairs of hands can bring is to make two of whatever entrée is on the menu, and freeze the second batch. This works especially well with one-dish meals like lasagna.

A Sophisticated Palate by Six Months Old

Another huge bonus of cooking with your kids is that when they help make the meal, they're more eager to actually eat it. Even the weird-looking healthy stuff. I was so touched when I got letters from moms across the country who wrote that when they cooked the recipes in *Skinny Italian*, their previously picky eaters gobbled them up. There was one precious little girl named Abigail who was two years old and would only eat chicken and olives—nothing but chicken and olives. I think if your kid will only eat two things, those are two pretty good things, especially considering the junk food alternatives, but her parents were desperate to introduce her to other flavors, textures, and food groups. My tagliatelle with peas and ham was a big hit with little Abigail, and they sent me pictures of her slurping down the noodles, *Lady and the Tramp*-style. (Hi Abby, baby doll!)

People always ask me if my girls are picky eaters, and the answer is a big fat "no." They will eat anything. There is literally not a single food they don't like. Even little Audriana likes pesto and spicy sauces and veggies. And I think it's because they've grown up in the kitchen.

Cooking with your kids helps them develop sophisticated palates. Not only are they more likely to eat things they had a hand in preparing, they're also learning to like healthier foods. Meals cooked from scratch have less hidden calories and added sugar than restaurant selections, fast food, or boxed dinners.

Super-sweet things like sugary snacks or foods made with high-fructose corn syrup can skew your child's taste buds to the point where they won't eat anything if it's not sweet. That's why pediatricians recommend that you introduce vegetables before fruits to babies, and limit the amount of juice they drink. And soda? Forget about it! One can of soda has about 10 teaspoons of sugar in it. In 2001, researchers from Harvard and Children's Hospital Boston completed a long-term study that showed a huge increase in childhood obesity for every extra serving per day of a sweetened beverage that kids drank. My kids drink milk and water by the bucketful.

Loving and then craving sweets is a vicious cycle you don't want your kids to have any part of. And you can control it from the minute they can eat solid food. When you're introducing new foods, don't be afraid of herbs and spices. Get them used to crunchy and creamy, savory foods right away.

It's never too late to start. Get your kids in the kitchen with you and cook up a feast, but be sure to include some of the things they might normally try and pick out: mushrooms, garlic, onions, parsley. If they're really resistant, try mashing the new foods up at first and hiding them in the dish, until they've learned to love the flavor. If you involve them, make it fun, and show them how much you love it, too, they will embrace it, I promise.

Kid-Friendly Kitchen Jobs

★ ★ ★ ★

Measuring
Pouring
Scooping
Stirring
Adding ingredients
Breading
Garnishing

GIUDICE GIRLS GONE WILD

If you just thought about a certain practically pornographic video series, then shame on you! This is a family cookbook! Unlike some of the other "Housewives," I do not condone young girls stripping to bring in business to a car wash, old ladies in hot pants climbing up a pole to bring their sexy back, or videotaping yourself in any state of undress at any time. I'm old-school. I did not live with Joe until we got married. I do my own child-raising, cleaning, and of course, cooking. But my girls are dying to take over this cookbook, and I promised them at least one chapter, so here we go . . .

Gia Giudice

Hi, I'm Gia, and I'm nine years old. I like dancing, acting, modeling, and doing almost anything with my mom . . . except when she's annoying me. Which thankfully isn't that often. I've been to Italy three times and my favorite city is Milan because of all the fashion there, not because it's part of my sister's name. And *puh*-lease, stop asking me what my middle name is because I don't have one. None of us do. It's some weird Italian thing.

My mom said I have to tell you my favorite recipe. I have lots of them, but if I had to pick one, I guess it would be Grilled Sausage & Peppers. I like when we use red, green, and yellow bell peppers. Those are the peppers that aren't hot, so your kids will probably like them, but I like the hot peppers, too.

P.S. If you make two batches, you can put the leftovers in the refrigerator, and you'll have delicious sandwiches the next day. —Gia

Gia's Grilled Sausage & Peppers

Makes 4 to 6 servings

Some people serve this over rice or pasta, but we like it with Italian bread. And you can use hot sausage if you like that kind better.

3 tablespoons extra-virgin olive oil

3 medium onions, cut into
½-inch-wide strips

1 red bell pepper, seeded and
cut into ½-inch-wide strips

1 yellow bell pepper, seeded and
cut into ½-inch-wide strips

1 green bell pepper, seeded and
cut into ½-inch-wide strips

2 garlic cloves, minced

2 tablespoons chopped fresh
Italian parsley

2 teaspoons dried oregano

Salt and freshly ground
black pepper

6 links sweet Italian sausage
(about 1¼ pounds), each
pierced with a fork

1. Build a hot fire in an outdoor grill. (Or, position a rack about 6 inches from the source of heat and preheat the broiler.)

2. Heat the oil in a large skillet over medium heat. Add the onions, red, yellow, and green peppers, and the minced garlic. Cover and cook until the vegetables soften a little, about 5 minutes. Uncover and cook, stirring occasionally, until the vegetables are tender, but not mushy, about 15 minutes. Stir in the parsley and oregano, and season with salt and pepper. Cook for 2 minutes to marry the flavors. Remove from the heat and cover to keep warm.

3. Meanwhile, lightly oil the grill grate. Place the sausages on the grill and cover. Grill, turning occasionally, until the sausages are browned and show no sign of pink when pierced in the center with the tip of a sharp knife, about 10 minutes. (Or broil the sausages for the same length of time.)

4. Transfer the peppers to a platter, top with the sausages, and serve hot.

S SKINNY VARIATION

Substitute turkey sausages for the pork.

Gabriella Giudice

I'm Gabriella, and I'm six years old. My room is pink Paris, and has the Eiffel Tower on the wall, and I have poodle pillows on my bed. My favorite dinner is Chicken Parmigiana because it tastes so good and my mom lets me roll the chicken in the breadcrumbs. She says to tell you that you can also use veal instead of chicken, but I like chicken the best.

P.S. My mom says if you want to save time, you can use spaghetti sauce from a jar. We won't tell anyone. Just make sure it's the good kind. —Gabriella

Gabriella's Chicken Parmigiana

Makes 6 servings

My mommy says to put the chicken on top of pasta when you bring it to the table. She says you can use any kind of spaghetti or long noodles, but I like angel hair the best.

6 (5-ounce) boneless and skinless
   chicken breast halves
1 teaspoon salt
¼ teaspoon freshly ground
   black pepper
⅔ cup all-purpose flour
3 large eggs
1 cup dry Italian-seasoned
   breadcrumbs
½ cup extra-virgin olive oil,
   plus more for the dish
3½ cups The Quickie Tomato
   Sauce (page 22)
2 cups (8 ounces) shredded
   fresh mozzarella cheese
   (freeze the cheese for 1 hour
   to firm before shredding)
½ cup (2 ounces) freshly grated
   Parmigiano-Reggiano cheese,
   plus more for serving
1 pound angel hair pasta
2 tablespoons chopped fresh
   Italian parsley, for garnish

1. Position a rack in the center of the oven and preheat the oven to 400°F. Lightly oil a 15 x 10-inch baking dish. Bring a large pot of lightly salted water to a boil over high heat.

2. One at a time, place half a chicken breast between two plastic storage bags. Pound with the flat side of a meat pounder or a rolling pin until the meat is about ½-inch thick. Season the chicken with the salt and pepper.

3. Place the flour in a shallow bowl. In a second shallow bowl, beat the eggs with 2 tablespoons of water. Place the breadcrumbs in a third bowl. Place a platter next to the breadcrumbs.

4. One at a time, coat the chicken with flour, shaking off the excess flour. Dip in the beaten egg mixture to coat, letting the excess egg drip back into the dish. Now roll in the breadcrumbs. Place on the platter. Let the breaded chicken stand for 10 minutes to set the coating.

5. Heat the oil in a large skillet over medium heat. In batches, add the chicken to the skillet and cook, turning once, until golden brown on both sides, 5 to 6 minutes. Transfer the chicken to the prepared baking dish.

6. Pour the tomato sauce around the chicken in the baking dish. Sprinkle the mozzarella and Parmigiano cheeses over the chicken. Bake until the cheese melts, about 8 minutes.

Fabulicious!

7. Meanwhile, just before serving, add the pasta to the water and cook according to the package directions until al dente. Drain well.

8. Transfer the pasta to six deep bowls. Top each with equal amounts of the sauce and a chicken breast half. Sprinkle with the parsley. Serve hot, with extra grated Parmigiano cheese to pass.

S SKINNY VARIATION

Don't use the flour, eggs, or breadcrumbs, and do not bread the chicken. Sauté the chicken in a nonstick skillet over medium heat without any oil until browned on both sides and the chicken feels firm when pressed in the center, about 6 minutes. Transfer to the baking dish, and add the tomato sauce. Sprinkle each chicken breast half with 1 tablespoon freshly grated Parmigiano-Reggiano and omit the mozzarella.

Milania Giudice

My name is Milania, and I'm four years old, and I'm FABULOUS! My mom says I talk too loud, but THAT'S NOT TRUE! I love to play with my baby sister Audriana, but when I pick her up and carry her, my mom yells at me. She also gets mad when I wake her up, but Audriana doesn't want to ALWAYS be taking a nap! She wants to play with me! I TOLD YOU!

I'm a very good cooker, and I look like my mommy—FABULOUS! My favorite thing to cook is . . . I don't know. What is it? Gabriella, stop, it's MY TURN! My favorite thing to cook is lasagna. My mom lets me help with the layers and I make them all pretty. Lasagna is fun to make because it's so pretty and the cheese is good. You can put any kind of meat inside. Sometimes we use sausages that my daddy makes inside it. Sometimes we only use vegetables. But this way is THE BEST!

P.S. My mom says to make two batches of lasagna at the same time and then freeze one before you cook it, so you have it next time you're in a hurry. We're always in a hurry.—Milania

Audriana Giudice

It's me, Audriana, and I'm only one year old . . . GIA! STOP TALKING FOR AUDRIANA! . . . Milania, Mom said I could! She can't talk yet . . . THEN I WANT TO TALK FOR HER! NOT YOU! . . . Mom said *I* could. Go ask her . . . M-O-O-O-M!!! . . .

Now that Milania's gone, I'm going to tell you what Audriana likes to eat the best. She's still little, so she likes things all mashed up. Mom said her favorite is Creamy Polenta. You like polenta, don't you, Audriana? Yes you do, you're so cute. Fabulous! Fabulous! I'm coming, Mom, I'm coming! Geez!

P.S. A lot of people think polenta is a kind of pasta, but really it's cornmeal. Polenta is great with stew, meat, or all by itself. And babies love it!

Audriana's Creamy Polenta

Makes 4 servings

Hi, it's me Gabriella. Don't tell Gia I'm telling you this, but you can make polenta ahead of time then put it in the frigerator. Later, you heat it back up in the microwave for 5 minutes. Mom lets me fluff it with a fork then, but you have to be careful not to burn yourself. Ok, I'll talk to you later . . .

4 cups canned reduced-sodium chicken or vegetable broth
1 cup coarsely ground polenta or stone-ground yellow cornmeal
3 tablespoons unsalted butter
Salt

1. Bring 2½ cups of the broth to a boil in a heavy-bottomed medium saucepan over medium heat.

2. Whisk the cornmeal into the remaining 1½ cups of broth in a small bowl. Whisk this mixture into the saucepan and return to the boil, whisking constantly. Whisk in the butter. Reduce the heat to low. Simmer, whisking often, until the polenta is thick and creamy, 30 to 40 minutes. (The coarser the grind, the longer the polenta will take to cook.) If the polenta gets too thick, whisk in some hot water. Season with salt.

Fabulicious!

Alright, the girls are doing their chores now—Gia has to empty the dishwasher, Gabriella sweeps the floor, and Milania wipes the table off—so I'm back. Before we head into the next chapter, I wanted to give you two more quick, easy, and cheap meals that are perfect for moms on the go. Like me, like you . . . Really, is there a mom on earth that isn't constantly running somewhere?

Stella Pastina

★ ★ ★ ★ (S) (Q) ★ ★ ★ ★

Makes 4 servings

Stella means "star" in Italian, and *pastina* is "little pasta." I know you've seen the tiny star pasta in the grocery store and loved it but wondered what to do with it. I'll tell you! This is a really easy, flexible dish. You can leave it wet and serve it as a soup, or drain the broth for a creamy pasta dish. Any shape of dried tiny pastina pasta is fine, but my girls like stars the best (sometimes labeled *stelline* in the store), and they cook the quickest. This is a great meal to make with leftover chicken, but you can add any other meat or vegetables that you have on hand. If you don't have Italian cheese, you can use American cheese slices in a pinch.

3 cups canned reduced-sodium
    chicken broth
½ cup finely chopped carrot
1 cup star-shaped pastina
1 cup (½-inch dice) cooked chicken
⅓ cup shredded fresh mozzarella
    cheese (freeze the cheese for
    1 hour to firm before grating)
Freshly grated Parmigiano-
    Reggiano cheese, for serving

1. In a medium saucepan, bring the broth and carrot to a boil over medium heat.

2. Add the pastina and cook until tender, about 6 minutes. During the last minute or so, add the chicken to heat it through.

3. Remove from the heat and stir in the mozzarella. Ladle into bowls and serve hot, with the grated Parmigiano cheese passed on the side.

Cavatelli with Red Sauce and Ricotta

* * * * (S) * * * *

Makes 6 servings

Cavatelli is a pasta (they look like tiny hot dog buns to me) that is made from ricotta cheese and flour so it won't be found with the dried pasta—it's either fresh or in some parts of the country, like Jersey, in the freezer section. If you can't find cavatelli at your local store, don't worry. I'll teach you how to make it from scratch in just a few pages.

You can serve this dish plain—it's great for lunch—or add Italian sausage, ground beef, or vegetables. The possibilities for personalizing it are endless, but here is the foundation.

12 ounces Homemade Cavatelli (see page 62), or use frozen cavatelli

3½ cups The Quickie Tomato Sauce (page 22), warmed

1¼ cups ricotta cheese

1. Bring a large pot of lightly salted water to a boil over high heat. Add the cavatelli and cook until they all float to the top, about 7 minutes. (If using frozen cavatelli, cook according to the package directions.)

2. Drain well. Do not rinse the pasta, even if your mother taught you to do so.

3. Transfer the pasta to a serving bowl. Add the sauce and mix gently. Serve in bowls, topping each serving with about 3 tablespoons of ricotta. Serve hot.

* * * Juicy Bits from Joe * * *

If you're gonna make this recipe with homemade cavatelli, I wouldn't put the ricotta on top if I was you. Tre will teach you how to make the cavatelli from scratch in a little bit, but know this: it already has lots of cheese in it. So, if you use the frozen cavatelli from the store, add the ricotta topping. If you make it yourself, leave it off 'cause you got enough cheese in there already.

Fabulicious!

CHAPTER 3

A PhD in Pasta

Curvy Italian bombshell and fashion icon Sophia Loren (one of my personal heroes) supposedly said of her fabulicious figure: "Everything you see, I owe to spaghetti." Even though she told CBS News in 2009 that it wasn't really her quote, I'm sticking to it. I love my pasta, and my pasta loves me.

You know you love pasta, too. In fact, you love it so much, when you were a kid, you glued it to construction paper and called it "art." And it is art. Call it what you want: spaghetti, pasta, macaroni, noodles . . . there's something magical about the simple combination of flour and just water or eggs. Especially when you make it yourself.

Not for nothing, dried pasta at the grocery store is delicious, cheap, and ready in minutes. Making your own pasta does take a little more time and effort. But the reward—especially when you do it with your family and friends—is so, so worth it.

> ✳✳✳ **Teresa's Tip** ✳✳✳
>
> A reminder of how fabulous people make pasta: add salt to the water right after it comes to a boil, but before you add the pasta; cook it until *al dente*, that is, until it's just a tiny, tiny bit tough in the center but still tender; and don't rinse your pasta after you drain it or you'll rob it of its natural ability to stick to the sauce.

The other night, we had three generations making homemade cavatelli in my kitchen: my ma, me, and my daughters. We had such a good time—joking about other times we'd made it, rolling it into different shapes. The girls loved it so much Gia took pictures with her little camera. When's the last time your kid took a picture of what you were cooking together for dinner? That—that's magic.

✳ ✳ ✳ How We Roll ✳ ✳ ✳

Now I'm not gonna lie, it is quicker to make pasta dough in a stand mixer with a dough hook instead of kneading it by hand (it's just not as sexy . . .). And while you know I like to do everything with my hands—I don't need toys to be happy—I do have to strongly suggest that you get a pasta machine to help you roll the pasta. You can technically use a rolling pin, but it's the one place you can really mess up your pasta—and we don't want to mess up our pretty pasta!

You can get an attachment for your stand mixer, but all you really need is a good, old-fashioned pasta roller with a hand crank. Electric or hand-powered, they're all called "pasta machines." You can find inexpensive manual ones just about anywhere online.

FROM HUMBLE FLOUR
TO FABULOUS HOMEMADE PASTA

Believe it or not, when it comes to making most all pasta from scratch—no matter if it's giant lasagna sheets or tiny corkscrews—you use the same basic recipe. That's right, just one recipe with just two things: flour and eggs. The ingredients are the same, the process is the same—even the tools are the same. The only difference in what you end up with is how you cut it. My recipe is, of course, called Perfect Pasta Dough. (I know some of you can't eat eggs, so hang tight, I'll give you not one, but *two* eggless pasta dough recipes in a just a bit!)

Before we begin though, I have to tell you: when you use fresh pasta, because it cooks so quickly, *make the sauce first*. Bring the pot of pasta water to a boil, then turn it to low while you prepare the sauce. Once the sauce is ready, bring the water back to a boil and cook your pasta.

Perfect Pasta Dough

Makes 1 pound

2 cups unbleached all-purpose
   flour, as needed
2 large eggs, beaten
¼ cup cold tap water

1. *To mix the pasta dough by hand:* Sift the flour into a mound on your work surface. Scoop out the center—now it's a volcano!—and add the displaced flour to the sides of the mound. Pour the eggs and cup cold water into the hole. Using your finger or a fork, gradually stir flour from the sides into the liquid. When most of the flour has been added, use your hands to knead the dough into a cohesive mass. If the dough is too dry, add more water, a tablespoon at a time. If it is too wet, add flour. Knead the dough on the work surface, adding more flour if necessary, until the dough is smooth and pliable, about 10 minutes. Do not add too much flour—the dough shouldn't be too stiff—remember that it has to be rolled out into thin sheets. Now move on to Step 3.

2. *To mix the dough in a heavy-duty standing mixer,* combine ¼ cup cold tap water and the eggs. Mix with the paddle attachment on low speed, gradually enough of the flour to make a soft dough that doesn't stick to the bowl. Change to the dough hook. On medium

✳ ✳ ✳ Juicy Bits from Joe ✳ ✳ ✳

Once you get a few batches of pasta under your belt, you can experiment with adding flavor right to the dough. You can cut up some fresh basil, or add some grated Parmigiano. You know that green pasta? That's from adding about ⅓ cup of cooked spinach, squeezed dry and chopped real good, to the dough. And if you wanna freak out your kids, you can even make black pasta. Tastes real good, especially with a cream sauce or a fish. You just get some squid ink from the fish guy and add a couple of tablespoons to the dough. Be careful though, that stuff does stain.

speed, knead the dough until smooth and supple, adding a little more flour or water by the tablespoon if necessary, about 8 minutes. Remember, the dough shouldn't be too stiff.

3. Shape the dough into a ball. Wrap in plastic wrap. Let stand at room temperature for 1 hour, no longer than 2 hours.

4. Attach your pasta machine to a kitchen counter. Cut the dough into four equal wedges. Shape each into a rectangle. Work with one portion at a time, keeping the remaining dough covered with the plastic.

Set the pasta machine to its widest setting. Dust the dough lightly with flour. Run the dough through the machine. Fold lengthwise and run through the machine 2 or 3 more times to knead and smooth the dough. Adjust the machine to the next thinnest setting. Run the dough through the machine twice, without folding it. Repeat with the next setting, and then the one after that, to make a long, thin strip of dough. If you want fettuccine, tagliatelle, or lasagna, the dough should be about the thickness of a nickel at this point, so stop. If you want ravioli, continue rolling on the next setting or two until the dough is as thick as a dime. Transfer the dough to a floured, tablecloth-covered table to dry slightly, just until the dough feels leathery, about 20 minutes. Don't let the dough dry too much, or it will crack.

5. *To cut the pasta with the machine:* Generously sprinkle a rimmed baking sheet with flour. For fettuccine, run each pasta strip through the widest cutters. For tagliatelle, run each pasta strip through the smaller cutters. (In America, fettuccine and tagliatelle are almost the same size, but in Italy, fettuccine is the thickest.) Transfer the pasta to the baking sheet, and toss with the flour to keep the strips from sticking.

To cut the pasta by hand: Use a knife or pizza wheel to cut long strips for fettuccine or tagliatelle. Cut the dough into large strips for lasagna and for ravioli.

The uncooked pasta can be made up to 6 hours ahead, covered loosely with plastic wrap and refrigerated.

6. To cook your pasta, bring a large pot of salted water to a boil. Add fresh pasta. Cook for just 1 to 2 minutes, depending on its thickness. As soon as the pasta floats, it's done!

*** **Teresa's Tip** ***

For most pasta shapes, like fettuccine, the dough should be as thick as a nickel. For ravioli, because it overlaps at the edges, the pasta should be only as thick as a dime.

Official Guide to Pasta Shapes

Long Noodles

They can be as long as you want them—usually 8 to 12 inches—but the width is what determines the kind of noodle you actually have:

* Pappardelle – ¾-inch wide
* Tagliatelle – ¼-inch wide
* Fettuccine – ⅙-inch wide
* Linguini – ⅛-inch wide

Pasta Sheets and Shapes

* Lasagna sheets: 3 x 13 inches
* Farfalle: 1 x 2-inch rectangles, pinched in the middle and twisted
* Fusilli: ¹⁄₁₆ x 3-inch strips, each wrapped around a pencil and allowed to dry

When in Rome . . .

Tagliatelle = tahl-yah-TELL-ay

Drying Time

After you've cut your dough into the shapes you want, let the pasta sit and dry for 15 minutes, before you throw it in a pot of water. This will keep the pasta from getting too soggy when it cooks. You can lay the noodles to dry all squiggly on a floured work surface (that's how I like to do it), or you can hang them all neat and individual anywhere you find room in your kitchen: on the back of your kitchen chairs (you might want to put a floured cloth down first), a horizontal broom handle, a clothesline . . . Or you can get one of those wooden pasta drying trees pretty cheap.

Different Tools for Cutting Pasta

* Pasta machine attachment
* Kitchen knife
* Pizza cutter
* Pastry roller
* Cookie cutters
* Rim of a glass
* Pasta/Ravioli press

Sexy Chick Eggless Pasta

Makes 1 pound

As promised, here is an eggless pasta dough. You might need to add a little olive oil to the noodles before you cook them to keep them from sticking, but paired with a delicious sauce, no one will know you only used flour, water . . . and a little bit of magic.

1 cup semolina (also called pasta flour)
1 cup unbleached all-purpose flour, plus more as needed
2/3 cup warm water

1. *To mix the pasta dough by hand:* Sift the semolina and flour into a mound on your work surface. Scoop out the center—now it's a volcano!—and add the displaced flour to the sides of the mound. Pour the warm water into the hole. Using your finger or a fork, gradually stir flour from the sides into the water. When most of the flour has been added, use your hands to knead the dough into a cohesive mass. If the dough is too dry, add more water, a tablespoon at a time. If it is too wet, add flour.

Knead on the work surface, adding more flour if necessary, until the dough is smooth and pliable, about 10 minutes. Do not add too much flour—the dough shouldn't be too stiff—remember that it has to be rolled out into thin sheets. Move to Step 3.

2. *To mix the dough in a heavy-duty standing mixer:* pour the warm water into the mixer bowl. Attach to the mixer and fit with the paddle attachment. Mix the semolina and flour together. With the machine on low speed, gradually add enough of the flour mixture to make a soft dough that doesn't stick to the bowl. Change to the dough hook. On medium speed, knead the dough until smooth and supple, adding more a little more flour or water by the tablespoon if necessary, about 8 minutes. Remember, the dough shouldn't be too stiff.

3. Shape the dough into a ball. Wrap in plastic wrap. Let stand at room temperature for 1 hour, no longer than 2 hours. Now continue from Step 4 in the instructions for Perfect Pasta Dough on page 55.

Homemade Cheesy Cavatelli

Makes about 1½ pounds, 6 to 8 servings

As Joe already told you, homemade cavatelli is a little different than regular pasta dough in that we make it with cheese instead of eggs. This is my kids' absolute favorite kind of pasta. Because it's so flavorful already, you don't need a really heavy sauce.

1 (15-ounce) container
ricotta cheese
2 cups unbleached all-purpose
flour, as needed

1. Put the ricotta in a large bowl. Gradually stir in just enough of the flour to make a soft dough that holds together. (I skip the spoon and use my hands.) Turn dough out onto a lightly floured work surface. Knead in enough of the remaining flour to make a smooth, pliable dough—the consistency should remind you of Play-Doh. This dough doesn't require as much kneading as other pasta.

2. Generously flour a rimmed baking sheet. Roll the dough into a thick log, and then cut into 16 equal portions. On a clean work surface, using clean, dry hands, roll 1 portion of dough under your palms into a long rope about ¼-inch thick. Cut the rope into 1-inch lengths. Here is where your Play-Doh training really comes in: Wrap a piece of dough around a pencil, spoon, or round chopstick until the sides almost meet—it will look like a little hot dog bun. Slide off and onto the baking sheet. (The cavatelli can be made up to 8 hours ahead, covered loosely with plastic wrap and refrigerated.)

3. Bring a large pot of lightly salted water to a boil over high heat. Carefully add the cavatelli and cook until they all float on the surface of the water, 1 to 3 minutes. Drain carefully (they are delicate and you don't want to smash them.) Serve hot.

✳ ✳ ✳ **My Ma's Middle Finger** ✳ ✳ ✳

Most people use a pencil or spoon to wrap their cavatelli, but my mama uses her middle finger to poke it into shape. You can also use a cavatelli machine, which you can find online, to literally crank them out.

My Manzo Ravioli

Makes about 4 dozen ravioli (6 to 8 servings)

This is not a quick dish, but it's so much fun, especially when you get kids or friends involved with the cutting and assembling! If you want a smoother, moister middle, you can use ground veal instead of ground beef.

Filling

1 tablespoon extra-virgin olive oil

8 ounces ground beef sirloin
  (93% lean)

1/2 medium onion, finely chopped

2 garlic cloves, minced

1/4 cup ricotta cheese

1/4 cup freshly grated Parmigiano-
  Reggiano cheese

1 large egg, beaten

1 tablespoon finely chopped fresh
  Italian parsley

1/2 teaspoon dried oregano

1/4 teaspoon salt

1/8 teaspoon freshly ground
  black pepper

Perfect Pasta Dough (page 55)

1 large egg, beaten

3 1/2 cups The Quickie Tomato
  Sauce (page 22), warmed

1/2 cup ricotta cheese, at room
  temperature, for serving

Chopped fresh basil, for serving

Freshly grated Parmigiano-
  Reggiano cheese, for serving

1. To make the filling, heat the oil in a large skillet over medium heat. Add the ground sirloin, onion, and garlic. Cook, stirring occasionally, breaking up the beef well with the side of a spoon, until it loses its raw look, 5 to 7 minutes. Transfer to a bowl and let cool slightly.

2. Add the ricotta, Parmigiano, egg, parsley, oregano, salt and pepper to the bowl with the beef and stir well to blend. Be sure that the meat is really well crumbled.

3. Generously dust 2 baking sheets with flour. If rolling out the pasta by hand, cut it into long strips about 4 inches wide. If using a pasta machine, shape each portion of dough into a rectangle before running it through the rollers so its final width is about 4 inches. Place a

* * * **Teresa's Tip** * * *

Need to save some time on the rolling and cutting? Try a ravioli press or mold: it looks like a flat, metal ice cube tray with fancy cutouts. You roll a large piece of dough over the whole thing, spoon filling into each space, add another sheet of dough, then smoosh closed with a rolling pin. Make sure you have enough flour on the press though, so the ravioli pop right out.

Fabulicious!

pasta strip on the work surface. Cut it in half vertically. Set one strip aside. With the longest side of the remaining pasta strip parallel to the work surface, space scant teaspoons of the filling 1 1/2 inches apart, about 1/2 inch from the bottom of the strip. Using a small pastry brush, paint beaten egg around all four sides of each portion of the filling. Top with the reserved pasta strip. Press firmly around each portion of filling, pressing out the air and adhering the two pasta strips to each other. Using a pizza wheel or fluted pastry cutter, cut around each portion of meat filling to make squares, or use a juice glass to make circles. (We're doing this with cheese ravioli in these photos!) Transfer to the baking sheet and toss with the flour. Repeat with the remaining pasta and filling. (The ravioli can be prepared up to 8 hours ahead, covered loosely with plastic wrap and refrigerated.)

4. Bring a large pot of lightly salted water to a boil over high heat. Carefully add the ravioli and cook until they all float to the surface of the water, 2 to 3 minutes. Drain carefully in a colander.

5. Place equal amounts of the ravioli in deep soup bowls, topping each with the tomato sauce, a dollop of ricotta, and a sprinkle of basil. Serve hot, with grated Parmigiano passed on the side.

✳ ✳ ✳ Juicy Bits from Joe ✳ ✳ ✳

Since so many recipes in here are named for actual people, you might think this one is in honor of Tre's co-stars Caroline or Dina from *The Real Housewives of New Jersey*. But it's not. We call it "manzo" ravioli because that's what it is: in Italian, "manzo" means "beef." Fun fact, huh? But do me a favor and don't call either of them "Mrs. Beef" next time you see them (although go ahead with Albie and Christopher …). And "Giudice"? It means "a judge" in Italian. I'm just sayin' …

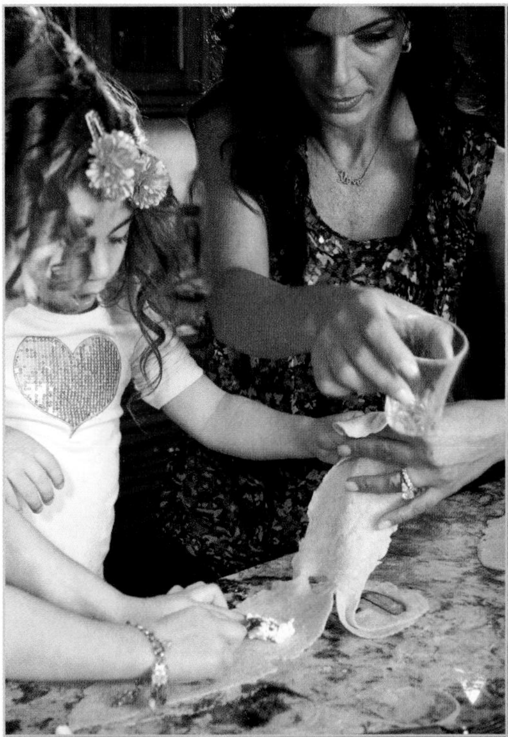
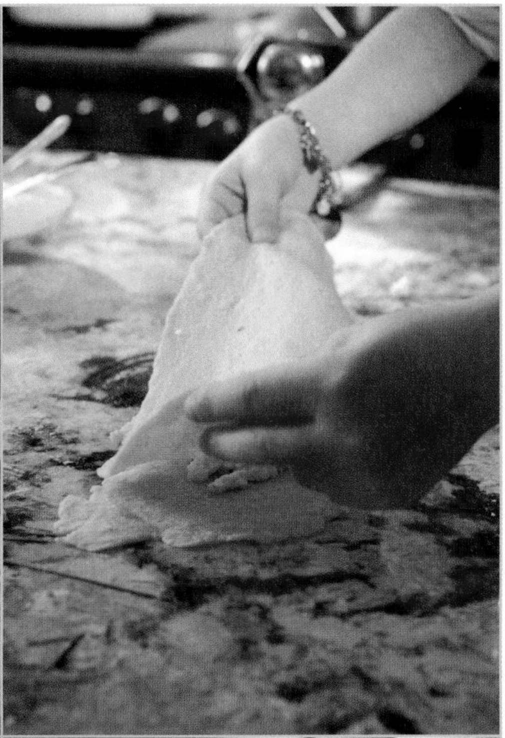
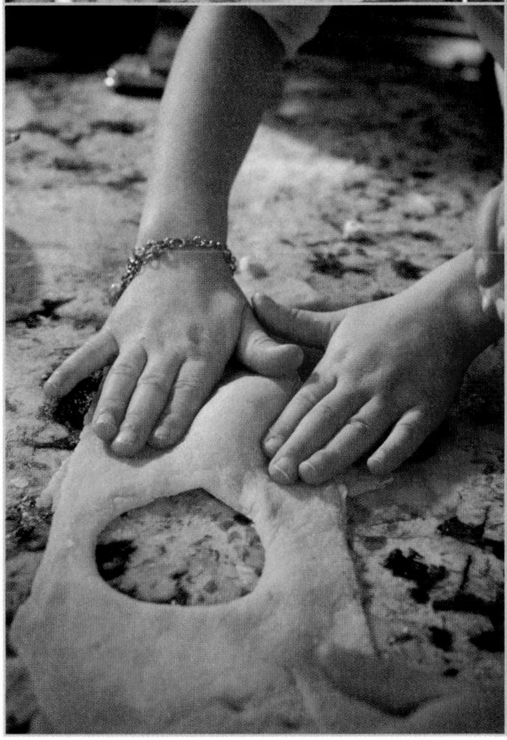
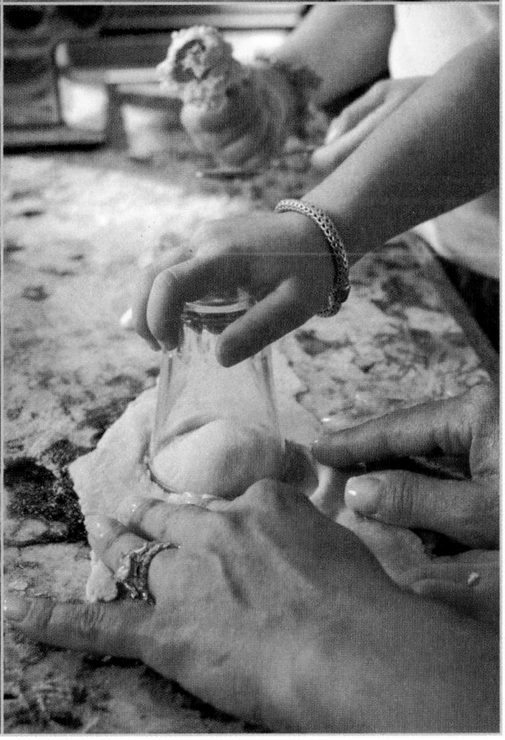

CHAPTER 4:

Bread from Heaven

Since we're on a make-it-yourself kick, I had to do a chapter on home-made Italian bread. Even if you've never tried to make bread before, you have to try these recipes—for the amazing way they will make your house smell alone!

I have no actual proof of this, but I would bet that Italian bread is the most popular bread on the planet. It's so easy to make—just flour, yeast, salt, and water—and so moist and delicious. French bread is good, but it's long, thin, and crusty (like a lot of the "Housewives" I know). A good Italian loaf is 18-inches long, 10-inches thick, and super porous. Technically, it's because the yeast is allowed to give off lots of gas to create those spongy holes in the bread, but I'll tell you from an eating standpoint, we make our bread that way because it's best for soaking up juicy toppings like olive oil and tomatoes.

I'm going to give you my great-grandmother's recipe for a Rustic Italian Loaf, plus a Fabulicious Focaccia, and a quick pizza crust dough recipe. Where's the ciabatta recipe? Not here, since it's not a traditional Italian bread. Believe it or not, ciabatta was invented as sort of a marketing gimmick in the 1980s. It was created in Italy, at least—by bread bakers who were upset that the French baguette was stealing all their business. So they came up with this funny, flat little loaf that's way too thin for sandwiches, hard to cut, and looks nothing like the Italian word it was named for: a slipper. It's good bread, sure, and the plan worked. But it's just not in my family's box of passed-down recipes.

Fabulicious!

My grandmother, nicknamed "Teresa," with my mom in 1954.

* * * A Rosa By Any Other Name * * *

My mother, Antonia Campiglia Gorga, was raised by her grandmother (my great-grandma Rosa) because her father left when she was a baby (he went to Venezuela and never came back . . . bastard!), and her own mom (also named Rosa) died when my mom was only ten years old. A month later, her grandfather died in his bed of a broken heart for losing his only daughter. Because both my great-grandma and grandma were named "Rosa," my grandmother's nickname became "Teresa." That's who I was named after. My dad wanted to honor her because he never got to meet her.

If you saw us visiting my hometown in Italy on the *The Real Housewives of New Jersey,* you know Sala Consilina is a rustic town built right into the mountains. I bet there's not an electric bread machine within a hundred miles! People (and not just Andy Cohen) always ask me how I have such great, muscular arms. I don't lift weights. I lift babies and bake bread. Want an old-school Italian workout? The only kitchen utensils we use for making our bread is a wooden spoon and the hands God gave us. Work it, Sweetheart!

* * * Knead Me * * *

In case no one ever taught you how to "knead," allow me. The trick is to dig into the dough with the heel of your hand, then push it away from you. Grab it back, flirt with it a little, fold it over, then shove it away again. (Somehow I knew you'd be good at this!)

Rosa's Rustic Italian Loaf

Makes 2 loaves

2 (¼-ounce) packages
    (4½ teaspoons) instant or
    quick-rise yeast
2 cups cold tap water
5½ cups unbleached all-purpose
    flour, as needed
2 teaspoons salt
Extra-virgin olive oil, for the bowl
    and baking sheet

1. *To make the bread by hand:* Combine the yeast with water in a large mixing bowl. Stir in 2 cups of flour and the salt. Gradually stir in enough of the remaining flour to make a dough that is too stiff to stir. Cover with a damp kitchen towel and let stand for 10 minutes. Then, turn the dough out onto a floured work surface. Knead, adding more of the flour as needed, until the dough is smooth, springy, and tacky to the touch, about 8 minutes. Do not add too much flour—as long as the dough isn't sticking to your hands or the work surface, there is enough.

To make the dough with a heavy-duty stand mixer: In the bowl of the mixer, combine the yeast with the cold water. Attach the bowl to the mixer and fit with the paddle attachment. With the machine on low speed, add 2 cups of flour and the salt. Gradually add enough of the remaining flour to make a dough that comes together and doesn't stick to the bowl. Wrap the top of the bowl with a damp towel and let stand for 10 minutes. Then, remove the paddle attachment and attach the dough hook. Knead the dough on medium speed,

∗ ∗ ∗ Bread Butts ∗ ∗ ∗

Ever wish you could do something with that extra bread "butt" that got too hard to eat instead of just throwing it away? You can cut the bread into cubes and freeze them in a freezer bag for up to six months. Once you have 6 cups of cubed bread, you have exactly what you need to cook up a batch of homemade croutons!

adding more flour as needed, until the dough is soft, springy, and tacky to the touch, about 8 minutes. Do not add too much flour—as long as it doesn't stick to the bowl, it has enough flour.

2. Lightly oil a large bowl. Shape the dough into a ball. Place the dough in the bowl and turn to coat the dough with oil, leaving the dough smooth-side up. Cover the bowl with a damp kitchen towel. Let stand in a warm, draft-free place until the dough doubles in volume (it's ready when you stick your finger an inch or so into the dough, and the indentation remains), about 1 1/2 hours.

3. Turn the dough back onto the floured surface and punch it (see why I'm such a good bread baker? Just kidding!) to get the air out. Then knead it for 2 minutes. Cut the dough in half, and form each into a ball. Place on the work surface and cover with the damp towel. Let stand for 10 minutes.

4. Lightly oil a large baking sheet. One at a time, shape each portion of dough into whatever loaf shape you want: round, oval, or long. The thing to remember is to stretch the dough as you make the shape so the surface looks taut. Transfer the loaves to the baking sheet and cover with the damp towel. Let stand in a warm place until the dough doubles in volume, about 1 hour.

5. Meanwhile, position a rack in the center of the oven and preheat thoroughly to 425°F. (The oven must be good and hot, so give it at least 20 minutes.)

6. Uncover the loaves. Using a sharp, thin-bladed knife, cut a shallow X in the top of the round loaf or a couple of diagonal slashes in the top of an oval or long loaf. Dust the tops of the loaves with flour. Bake for 10 minutes. Reduce the temperature to 350°F. Continue baking until the loaves are golden brown and sound hollow when you tap them on the bottoms with your knuckles, 20 to 25 minutes. Let cool for 20 minutes before slicing . . . if you can wait that long.

Fabulicious Focaccia

Makes 1 loaf

This is my favorite bread because it's so delicious and juicy! Unlike the Rustic Italian Loaf, you kind of make focaccia in two parts: first you make a batter; then when you add flour to it, it becomes more of a dough. Traditionally, focaccia bread only has olive oil, rosemary, and coarse salt on top. You can add a million different things, though: cheese, olives, sautéed onions, garlic . . .

7 tablespoons extra-virgin olive oil, divided

2 tablespoons granulated sugar

2 teaspoons instant or quick-rise yeast

1 cup cold tap water

3½ cups unbleached all-purpose flour, as needed

1½ teaspoons plain or table salt

2 tablespoons finely chopped fresh rosemary

1 teaspoon kosher or other coarse salt, for topping

1. *To make the dough by hand:* In a large mixing bowl, combine ¼ cup of the olive oil, the sugar, and the yeast with the cold water. Using a sturdy wooden spoon, stir in 2 cups of flour and the salt to make a batter. Stir in one direction until the batter is very elastic (if you pull up the spoon, the batter will stretch at least 6 inches before it breaks), at least 5 minutes, or 10 minutes if you want a great upper-body workout.

Gradually stir in enough of the remaining flour to make a dough that is too stiff to stir. Turn the dough out onto a lightly floured work surface. Knead, adding more flour as needed, until the dough is smooth, springy, and tacky to the touch, about 5 minutes. Do not add too much flour—as long as the dough isn't sticking to your hands or the work surface, there is enough flour. Go to step 3.

✳ ✳ ✳ Teresa's Tip ✳ ✳ ✳

You need 2 teaspoons of yeast for this recipe, and those little individual envelopes contain 2¼ teaspoons. Measure out only 2 teaspoons and then just toss the extra. Of course, if you buy the yeast in a jar or in bulk, then just scoop out what you need.

2. *To make the dough with a heavy-duty stand mixer:* In the bowl of the mixer, combine ¼ cup of the olive oil, the sugar, and the yeast with the cold water. Attach the bowl to the mixer and fit with the paddle attachment. With the machine on low speed, add 2 cups of flour and the salt. Mix on low speed until the dough is very elastic (if you turn off the machine and lift up the paddle, the batter will stretch at least 6 inches before it breaks), about 5 minutes.

Gradually stir in enough of the flour to make a dough that comes together and does not stick to the bowl. Remove the paddle attachment and attach the dough hook. Knead the dough on medium speed, adding more flour as needed, until the dough is soft, springy, and tacky to the touch. Do not add too much flour—as long as it doesn't stick to the bowl, it has enough flour.

3. Generously oil a large bowl with 1 tablespoon of the remaining oil. Shape the dough into a ball. Add to the bowl and turn to coat with oil, leaving the dough smooth-side up.

Cover with a damp kitchen towel. Let stand in a warm, draft-free place until the dough has doubled in volume, about 1½ hours.

4. Lightly oil a 13 x 9-inch rimmed baking sheet. Turn out the dough onto the baking sheet. Using your hands, stretch the dough to fill the baking sheet. If the dough springs back too much, cover the dough with the damp kitchen towel and let rest for a few minutes, then try again. When the sheet is filled, cover the dough with the damp towel and let stand in a warm place until puffy, about 30 minutes.

5. Position a rack in the bottom third of the oven and preheat to 400°F. Using your fingertips (unless you have long nails or don't want to ruin your manicure) or the handle of a wooden spoon, poke indentations in the top of the dough to make those delicious dimples. Brush the top with the remaining 2 tablespoons of oil. Sprinkle with the rosemary and salt.

6. Bake until the focaccia is golden brown, about 20 minutes. Cool slightly. Cut into squares and serve warm or at room temperature.

When in Rome . . .

Focaccia = fo-KAH-cha

Pronto Presto Pizza Dough

* * * * **Q** * * * *

Makes 2 balls of dough

In *Skinny Italian*, I taught you my family's secret recipe for the best pizza pie dough this side of Salerno. However, it does take some time, and it's best when used simply as a pizza crust. I wanted to give you a quicker, more versatile version in this book for those times when you're in a hurry—really, is there any time when you're not? You can top this and make any kind of pizza you want, but I'm also going to have you use it in later recipes for a calzone and pie. (I know I'm all about using your hands, but you will need a stand mixer to make this dough or it really won't be very pronto or presto.)

2 2/3 cups bread flour,
    as needed

2 tablespoons extra-virgin
    olive oil

1 (1/4-ounce) package
    (2 1/4 teaspoons) instant
    or quick-rise yeast

1 teaspoon salt

1 cup hot tap water
    (no more than 130°F)

1. In the bowl of a heavy-duty stand mixer, combine 1 1/4 cups of flour, the olive oil, yeast, and salt. Add the hot water. Attach the bowl to the mixer and fit with the paddle attachment. Mix on low speed until the batter is elastic, about 4 minutes. Add enough of the remaining flour to make a dough that cleans the sides of the bowl. Remove the paddle attachment and attach the dough hook. Knead on medium speed until the dough is smooth and supple, about 4 minutes.

2. Shape the dough into a ball. Transfer to a large bowl (no need to oil the bowl) and cover with a damp towel. Let stand in a warm, draft-free place until the dough doubles in volume, about 30 minutes.

3. Cut the dough in half and shape each half into a ball. Use immediately.

* * * Juicy Bits from Joe * * *

So you just made this dough and you can't wait for a recipe—you wanna make a pizza now, huh? Roll out the dough into a circle or square or whatever. Make it however thick you want. I like mine thin. Put a little sauce on there, your favorite toppings—some prosciutto maybe, some sausage, fresh mozzarella—then cook it at 450°F until it's light brown, about 10 minutes.

CHAPTER 5

The Lighter Side of Life

I wanted to cover all aspects of our family cooking, not just dinners. So here is my much-requested lunch chapter! Of course, you can make these recipes anytime, but they are perfect for a midday meal: they're light, easy to make, perfect for smaller portions (or solo lunch dates), and fabulicious!

No Bread Left Behind Croutons

Makes 6 cups

Feel free to add more herbs, garlic, or even cheese to your croutons. For garlicky croutons, add 2 minced garlic cloves to the herb-oil mixture. For "Parm" croutons, during the last 5 minutes of baking, sprinkle the croutons with ¼ cup freshly grated Parmigiano-Reggiano cheese.

½ loaf day-old Italian bread

⅓ cup extra-virgin olive oil

1 tablespoon finely chopped fresh Italian parsley

1 teaspoon dried oregano

1. Position a rack in the center of the oven and preheat the oven to 300°F.

2. Cut the bread into 1-inch slices. Remove the crust, if you wish. Cut the slices into 1-inch cubes (you should have about 6 cups). Transfer the bread cubes to a large bowl, preferably one with a lid.

3. In a glass measuring cup, combine the oil, parsley, and oregano and whisk to blend. Drizzle the herb-oil mixture over the bread cubes. Cover and shake until coated. (If you don't have a cover for the bowl, stir well to coat.)

4. Spread the cubes in a single layer on a rimmed baking sheet. Bake until golden brown, 15 to 20 minutes. Let cool. (The croutons can be frozen in an airtight container for up to 6 months. Thaw before using.)

Amazing Arugula Salad

★ ★ ★ ★ ⦿ **S** ⦿ **Q** ⦿ ★ ★ ★ ★

Makes 4 servings

You can serve this as a salad, or use it as a filling for a whole wheat pita or flat bread, or even on already-cooked pizza crust! If you like—and I do!—sprinkle pine nuts on top.

2 tablespoons freshly squeezed
 lemon juice

3 tablespoons extra-virgin olive oil

¼ cup (1 ounce) freshly grated
 Parmigiano-Reggiano cheese

Salt

6 ounces baby arugula, washed
 and dried

1 cup cherry or grape tomatoes,
 halved

1. Pour the lemon juice into a small bowl. Gradually whisk in the oil. Whisk in the Parmigiano cheese and season with salt.

2. Combine the arugula and tomatoes in a large bowl. Add the dressing and toss to coat. Serve immediately.

★ ★ ★ **Aruga-wha?** ★ ★ ★

Arugula has more names than Danielle. It's also called Italian cress, rugola, roquette, and rucola. But my favorite alias is used in Britain. They just call it "rocket." Love it.

Las Vegas Caesar Salad

★ ★ ★ ★ ⬤ S ⬤ Q ⬤ ★ ★ ★ ★

Makes 6 servings

Like almost everything in the famous city of neon lights, my own Caesar salad recipe is kind of a knock-off of the original, but in a lot of ways, much better. I'm not a huge fan of putting barely-cooked eggs in my salad, so my version is eggless. I do, however, love anchovies, so those stay. If anchovies skeeve you out and you want to cut them from the recipe, feel free—what happens in your kitchen, stays in your kitchen.

1 (2-ounce) can anchovy filets, drained and coarsely chopped

3 tablespoons balsamic vinegar

2 tablespoons freshly squeezed lemon juice

1 teaspoon Worcestershire sauce

1 garlic clove, minced

1/2 teaspoon salt

1/4 teaspoon dry mustard

1/8 teaspoon freshly ground black pepper

3/4 cup extra-virgin olive oil

1 head romaine lettuce, torn into bite-sized pieces, rinsed and dried

1 cup cherry or grape tomatoes, halved

1 1/2 cups No Bread Left Behind Croutons (page 81), or use store-bought croutons

1/2 cup (2 ounces) freshly grated Parmigiano-Reggiano cheese

1. Place half of the anchovies in a small mixing bowl and mash with a fork. Add the balsamic vinegar, lemon juice, Worcestershire sauce, garlic, salt, dry mustard, and pepper and whisk to combine. Gradually whisk in the oil. (The dressing can be made up to 1 day ahead, covered and refrigerated. Whisk again before using.)

2. Combine the lettuce and tomatoes in a large bowl. Add the dressing and toss to coat. Add the croutons, sprinkle with the cheese, and toss again. Serve immediately.

★ ★ ★ All Hail Who? ★ ★ ★

The Caesar is an Italian salad, but it has nothing to do with Julius Caesar . . . or ancient Italy, for that matter. While a Chicago chef, Giacomo Junia, claims to have invented the salad in 1903, most people believe it originated at Caesar Cardini's restaurant in Tijuana, Mexico in 1924. Cardini's family say that the salad was a spur-of-the-moment creation for hungry customers. To compensate for not having his regular salad ingredients, Cardini wheeled everything on a cart to the table and prepared it in front of the customers.

Roasted Portobello and Rosemary Salad

★★★★ S Q ★★★★

Makes 6 servings

If it's nice weather or you or your man is a grill master, you can always throw the mushrooms on the barbecue, but it's just as easy to cook them indoors under the broiler.

Extra-virgin olive oil

1 tablespoon balsamic vinegar

2 teaspoons chopped
    fresh rosemary

1 garlic clove, minced

⅛ teaspoon salt

⅛ teaspoon freshly ground
    black pepper

¼ cup plus 3 tablespoons
    extra-virgin olive oil

8 large portobello mushroom caps

8 ounces baby mixed greens,
    rinsed and dried

1. Position the broiler rack about 6 inches from the source of heat and preheat the broiler. Lightly oil the broiler pan.

2. In a small mixing bowl, whisk together the balsamic vinegar, rosemary, garlic, salt, and pepper. Gradually whisk in ¼ cup of the oil. Set the dressing aside.

3. Wipe the mushrooms clean with a damp cloth. Brush them all over with the remaining 3 tablespoons oil. Place on the broiler pan, smooth sides up, and broil until tender, about 12 minutes. Transfer mushrooms to a carving board. Cut the mushrooms into ½-inch-thick strips. Pour any juices into the dressing and whisk to blend.

4. Toss the greens with the dressing. Add the warm mushroom strips. Serve immediately.

Capri Salad Coupling

★ ★ ★ ★ (S Q) ★ ★ ★ ★

Makes 6 servings

The Italian island of Capri is famous for its caprese salad—a simple but delicious combination of tomatoes and fresh mozzarella. It's traditionally served cold, but it can be warmed up in the oven or served on bread as a sandwich. I'm giving you two recipes here, one for the spread-out-on-a-platter cold salad, and another for a warm, towers-of-tomato-and-cheese nirvana option.

2 tablespoons balsamic vinegar

½ teaspoon dried oregano

¼ cup extra-virgin olive oil

Salt and freshly ground black pepper

3 large heirloom or beefsteak tomatoes

8 ounces fresh mozzarella cheese

½ cup pitted and coarsely chopped Kalamata olives

¼ cup chopped fresh basil

Extra-virgin olive oil

1. To make the dressing, whisk together the balsamic vinegar and oregano in a small mixing bowl. Gradually whisk in the oil. Season with salt and pepper. Set aside.

2. Core the tomatoes and slice them crosswise for a total of eighteen ⅓-inch-thick rounds. Cut the mozzarella into six ¼-inch-thick slices, then cut each slice into thirds to make 18 pieces. The pieces will not all be the same size, which is fine.

3. *To make a cold plated salad:* Alternate and overlap the tomatoes and mozzarella on a platter. Drizzle with the dressing. Sprinkle with the olives and basil, and serve.

To make warm tomato-and-mozzarella stacks: Position a broiler rack about 8 inches from the source of heat and preheat the broiler. Lightly oil the broiler pan. For each serving, alternate and stack a tomato round, a piece of mozzarella, and a few chopped olives. Repeat, and finish with a third tomato slice and a third mozzarella slice on top (this will make 6 stacks). You will not use all of the olives. Place the stacks on the broiler pan. Broil until the mozzarella toppings are melted and lightly browned, about 3 minutes. The stacks should be warmed, not piping hot. Transfer each tomato and mozzarella stack to a dinner plate. Spoon the dressing over and around each stack, sprinkle with the remaining olives and the basil, and serve.

Genoa Love You Sandwich

★ ★ ★ ★ Q ★ ★ ★ ★

Makes 1 sandwich

Genoa is the place that perfected pesto—the delicious basis of this vegetarian sandwich.

2 slices Rosa's Rustic Italian Loaf or
    Fabulicious Focaccia (pages 74
    and 76), or use store-bought
1½ tablespoons Audriana's
    Creamy Pesto (page 24)
½ roasted red pepper, preferably
    Papà's Roasted Peppers (page
    26), cut to fit the bread
3 slices ripe heirloom
    or beefsteak tomato
2 ounces fresh mozzarella,
    thinly sliced
A few thin slices of onion

1. Place 1 slice of bread on the work surface, and spread with the pesto. Layer the red pepper, tomato slices, mozzarella, and onion on top. Cover with the remaining slice of bread. Cut in half and serve.

★ ★ ★ Slapping the Salami ★ ★ ★

You probably know Genoa for its salami, but did you know salami is actually a type of sausage? Fermented sausage. I won't tell you how it's made, but it's extra delicious because the pigs feed on wild Italian acorns and hazelnuts.

When in Jersey . . .
Sandwich = SANG-wich

Chicken Pesto Panini

* * * * (Q) * * * *

Makes 1 sandwich

This is a great way to introduce new flavors and foods—like roasted red peppers—to a picky eater because everything is packaged in a giant "grilled cheese" sandwich. Red bell peppers are sweet and a little fruity, but have the same texture as hotter peppers; they are great for little teeth, and for teaching kids not to be afraid of the pepper family.

P.S.: Technically just one sandwich is called a *panino*, but you can of course multiply this recipe for however many panini-crazed people you're cooking for.

2 slices Rosa's Rustic Italian Loaf or Fabulicious Focaccia (pages 74 and 76), or use store-bought

1½ tablespoons Audriana's Pesto (page 24) or store-bought olive pesto (tapenade) or sun-dried tomato pesto

2 ounces fresh mozzarella cheese, thinly sliced

1 precooked chicken tender (about 3 ounces), cut on the diagonal into 3 or 4 pieces

½ roasted red pepper, preferably Papà's Roasted Peppers (page 26), cut to fit the bread

A few arugula leaves or fresh spinach leaves

Extra-virgin olive oil, for brushing

1. Heat an electric panini grill according to the manufacturer's instructions. (For a stovetop method, see page 92.)

2. Spread the pesto on one side of each bread slice. Top one slice with half of the mozzarella, then the chicken, red pepper, and arugula. Place the remaining mozzarella atop the arugula. Cover with the remaining bread slice, pesto-side down. Lightly brush both sides of the sandwich with olive oil.

3. Place the sandwich in the grill and close the lid. Cook until the sandwich is golden brown and the cheese melts, about 5 minutes. Cut in half and serve.

> *** * * Teresa's Tip * * ***
>
> Another reason it's great to have lots of Papà's Roasted Peppers and Audriana's Pesto on hand in your fridge: you can use them to whip up a delicious sandwich in minutes! Every time I make either recipe, I double it just so I have extra for later.

Prosciutto Asparagi Panini

★ ★ ★ ★ ⟨ ♀ ⟩ ★ ★ ★ ★

Makes 1 sandwich

I was inspired to make this panini by the easiest appetizer ever: roasted asparagus stalks individually wrapped in prosciutto. While the two taste phenomenal together, picky eaters sometimes pass on the healthy green veggie stalks out of habit. I decided to slice them thin and hide—I mean *put*—them in a sandwich.

8 asparagus spears, roasted
   (see Roasted Asparagus alla
   Parmigiana, page 130)
2 slices Rosa's Rustic Italian Loaf or
   Fabulicious Focaccia (pages 74
   and 76), or use store-bought
2 ounces mozzarella cheese,
   thinly sliced
Freshly ground black pepper
2 ounces thinly sliced prosciutto
Extra-virgin olive oil, for brushing

1. Heat an electric panini grill according to the manufacturer's instructions. (For a stovetop method, see page 92.)

2. Slice the asparagus crosswise to fit the bread. Place one slice of bread on a work surface. Top with half of the mozzarella, then the asparagus. Season the asparagus with ground black pepper (you won't need salt because of the salty prosciutto). Top the asparagus with the prosciutto slices and finish with the remaining mozzarella. Cover with the remaining bread slice. Lightly brush both sides of the sandwich with olive oil.

3. Place the sandwich in the grill and close the lid. Cook until the sandwich is golden brown and the cheese melts, about 5 minutes. Cut in half and serve.

> *When in Rome . . .*
> Prosciutto = pro-SHOE-toh

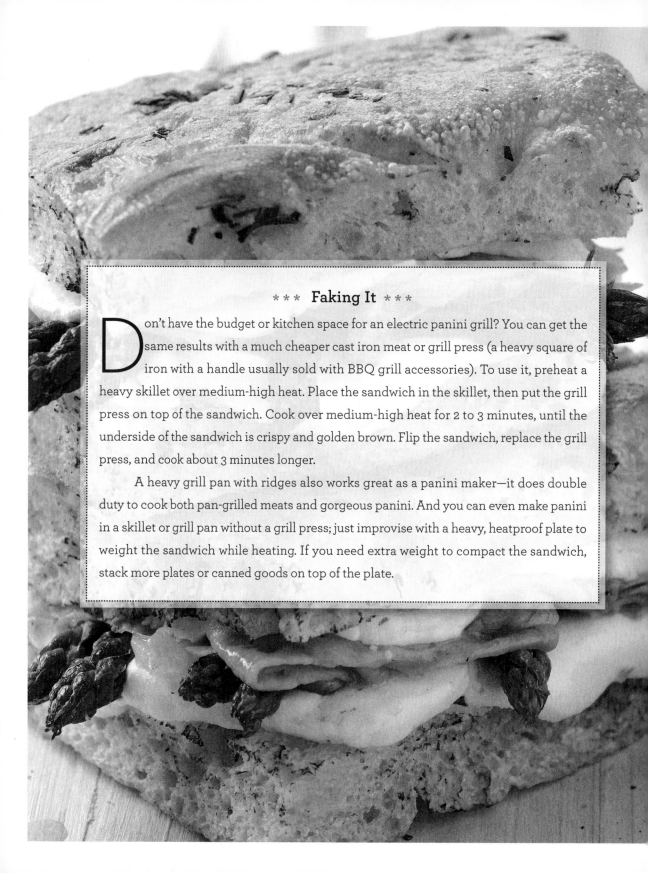

✳ ✳ ✳ Faking It ✳ ✳ ✳

Don't have the budget or kitchen space for an electric panini grill? You can get the same results with a much cheaper cast iron meat or grill press (a heavy square of iron with a handle usually sold with BBQ grill accessories). To use it, preheat a heavy skillet over medium-high heat. Place the sandwich in the skillet, then put the grill press on top of the sandwich. Cook over medium-high heat for 2 to 3 minutes, until the underside of the sandwich is crispy and golden brown. Flip the sandwich, replace the grill press, and cook about 3 minutes longer.

A heavy grill pan with ridges also works great as a panini maker—it does double duty to cook both pan-grilled meats and gorgeous panini. And you can even make panini in a skillet or grill pan without a grill press; just improvise with a heavy, heatproof plate to weight the sandwich while heating. If you need extra weight to compact the sandwich, stack more plates or canned goods on top of the plate.

Hot Roman Pasta Fagioli

★ ★ ★ ★ **Q** ★ ★ ★ ★

Makes 8 servings

Who doesn't love a hot Roman? This is one of my family's most favorite dishes. *Fagiolo* means "bean" in Italian, but the exact bean we use in this recipe has many names. In my house, we call them Romano beans, but you might see them labeled as Roman beans, cranberry beans, borlotti beans, or shell beans. You can make this dish as soupy as you want by adding or subtracting water.

2 large celery ribs, thinly sliced, leaves reserved

2 (15 ½-ounce) cans Roman beans, drained and rinsed

1 (14½-ounce) can reduced-sodium chicken broth

1 cup The Quickie Tomato Sauce (page 22)

3 large carrots, chopped

⅛ teaspoon red pepper flakes

2 cups small shell pasta

Salt

1. Combine 1 quart water with the celery leaves in a large, heavy pot and bring to a boil over high heat. (The leaves will flavor the water and turn it green.) Remove and discard the celery leaves.

2. Add the beans, broth, tomato sauce, celery, carrots, and red pepper flakes and bring to a boil. Reduce the heat to medium-low. Simmer until the vegetables are tender, about 30 minutes.

3. Add the pasta and cook until tender, about 15 minutes. If the soup gets too thick, thin it with hot water. Season with salt. Serve hot.

When in Rome . . .	*When in Jersey . . .*
Fagioli = fah-JOE-lee	Fagioli = fah-ZOOL

Gemelli Twists with Tomato Soffrito

✴ ✴ ✴ ✴ (**S**) ✴ ✴ ✴ ✴

Makes 4 to 6 servings

A *soffrito* is a combination of onion, carrots, and celery mixed with herbs, sautéed in olive oil, and used as a base for many Italian dishes. I add tomatoes and mix it with pasta to make a quick, meatless weeknight dinner that is easy on the budget.

3 tablespoons extra-virgin olive oil

1 medium onion, finely chopped

1 medium carrot, finely chopped

1 celery rib with leaves,
    finely chopped

2 garlic cloves, minced

8 ripe plum tomatoes, seeded
    and diced

2 sprigs fresh rosemary

2 tablespoons chopped fresh basil

1 teaspoon chopped fresh sage

1/2 cup tap water

Salt and freshly ground
    black pepper

1 pound gemelli pasta

1/4 cup chopped fresh
    Italian parsley

Freshly grated Parmigiano-
    Reggiano cheese, for serving

1. Heat the oil in a large saucepan over medium heat. Add the onion, carrot, celery, and garlic. Cook, stirring occasionally, until the onion is translucent, about 5 minutes.

2. Stir in the tomatoes, rosemary sprigs, chopped basil, sage, and water. Cook, stirring often, until the tomatoes have cooked into a thick, chunky sauce, about 15 minutes. Season with salt and pepper. Discard the rosemary sprigs.

3. Meanwhile, bring a large pot of lightly salted water to a boil over high heat. Add the pasta and cook according to the package directions until al dente. Drain well.

4. Return the pasta to the pot. Add the sauce and parsley and mix well. Serve hot, with the grated Parmigiano passed on the side.

CHAPTER 6

Antipasto: Come On-A My House

Every culture and religion has its own holidays, feasts, and festivals, and we Italians are no exception. We love a good party! And I really don't think we go over the top. (Alright, so maybe you didn't have Marie Antoinette serving sushi off her dress at your baby's christening, but that's probably just because you didn't think of it.) If it's a special occasion—especially a once-in-a-lifetime event like a bar (or bat) mitzvah, *quinceañera*, or (hopefully) a wedding, you should go all-out.

But you definitely don't have to break the bank to put out a good spread. Italians are known for our delicious antipasti platters, and I'm going to teach you how to arrange a perfect one, and how to make some of our traditional appetizers, all of them great for big events or small family gatherings. Where there's people, there should be food!

PARTY PLATTERS

There's really no big secret to creating an antipasti platter. I know the stores would like you to think there is so you can spend $75 on a plastic tray full of sliced deli meat, but you can easily make it at home. There's no special plate you need. No special way of presenting it. Just lay everything out real nice, overlap the layers, roll it if you can, add bits of fresh parsley or hard-boiled eggs cut in half for a garnish, and you're done!

Audriana's 1st birthday

Audriana's Christening

There are a million variations, but at a minimum, gatherings usually have:

The Salami Platter

Overlapping slices of salami, prosciutto, coppa, soppressa, and/or mortadella. You can cut them as thin or as thick as you like.

The Crostini Platter

Crostini means "little toasts" in Italian, and that's exactly what they are: toasted bread slices. You can either top them individually ahead of time with diced, spiced veggies (bruschetta), or set them next to a bowl of dip for your guests to serve themselves. Another option is to use *grissini,* thin Italian breadsticks, either for dipping or individually wrapped in a slice of prosciutto.

The Marinated or Stuffed Veggies Platter

Stuffed olives, garlic bites, roasted peppers . . . the possibilities are endless. Papà's Roasted Peppers (page 26) is a great place to start.

The Fritto Platter

OK, so *fritto* means "fried," and it's not very healthy, but we're talking a couple appetizers here, not a three-pound main meal. In just a sec, I'm going to give you my recipe for deep-fried cauliflower.

I'm going to teach you how to make my favorite appetizers—even my famous calamari! But first, let's take it nice and easy . . .

Olive Juice Bread Bath

* * * * Q * * * *

Makes about 1 cup (6 to 8 servings)

Every table should have a glorious bowl of seasoned olive oil to dip bread, crostini, or really anything into. Throw away your tub of partially hydrogenated margarine scariness, and enjoy the pure delight of nature's own olive juice. (And of course, you must mouth the words "olive juice" to the person next to you every time you dunk—even if you're standing next to one of your in-laws. It's my family rule.).

¼ cup (1 ounce) freshly grated
   Parmigiano-Reggiano cheese
2 tablespoons finely chopped
   fresh Italian parsley
1 tablespoon dried oregano,
   crushed
4 garlic cloves, minced
2 teaspoons freshly ground
   black pepper
1 teaspoon salt
½ cup extra-virgin olive oil
¼ cup balsamic vinegar
Crusty bread, for serving

1. In a small mixing bowl, combine the cheese, parsley, oregano, garlic, pepper, and salt; stir to blend. Transfer half of the cheese mixture to a wide, shallow serving bowl.

2. Pour the oil over the cheese mixture in the serving bowl, then drizzle with the vinegar. Sprinkle the remaining cheese mixture on top. Serve with the bread for dipping.

> *** * * Teresa's Tip * * ***
>
> Any leftovers can be refrigerated for another meal, or saved for an instant salad dressing.

Love Me Tender Eggplant Caponata

★ ★ ★ ★ S Q ★ ★ ★ ★

Makes 6 servings

A *caponata* is a cooked eggplant dish you can pile on top of toasted bread slices, or serve as a spread. There are thousands of variations. (For those of you playing at home, my Caponata Bruschetta in *Skinny Italian* had olives and different herbs.) You can serve caponata immediately, or let it cool to room temperature first. My best secret: make it the night before and store it in the fridge. The flavors will get to know one another, mingle a bit, let their guard down, and you will have an even better dish the next day.

1 large eggplant (1½ pounds),
   trimmed
¼ cup extra-virgin olive oil
1 small red onion, chopped
2 teaspoons chopped fresh thyme
1 large ripe tomato, seeded
   and diced
2 tablespoons balsamic vinegar
2 tablespoons drained capers
Salt and freshly ground
   black pepper
3 tablespoons chopped fresh
   Italian parsley
1 garlic clove, minced

1. Cut the eggplant in half lengthwise. Using a melon baller or teaspoon, scoop out the visible clusters of seeds. Cut the eggplant, with the skin on, into 1-inch cubes.

2. Heat the oil in a large skillet over medium-high heat. Add the onion and cook, stirring occasionally, until softened, about 3 minutes. Add the cubed eggplant and thyme. Cook, stirring often, until the eggplant is softened but not mushy, about 4 minutes. If the mixture in the skillet dries out, add a few tablespoons of water, but not more oil.

3. Stir in the tomato, balsamic vinegar, and capers. Reduce the heat to medium. Cook, stirring often, until the eggplant is completely tender, about 3 minutes. Season with salt and pepper.

4. Remove from the heat. Stir in the parsley and garlic. Serve warm, or let cool to room temperature. (The caponata can be made, covered and refrigerated, up to 5 days ahead.)

Cauli-Flowers

★ ★ ★ ★ Q ★ ★ ★ ★

Makes 6 to 8 servings

These are Italian party favorites—like little clouds of fried heaven. And they're even better with freshly grated Parmigiano-Reggiano sprinkled over the top.

Olive oil, for deep-frying

1 large egg

½ cup water

1 cup all-purpose flour

1 tablespoon finely chopped fresh Italian parsley, plus more for garnish

½ teaspoon salt

1 head cauliflower, trimmed and cut into bite-sized florets

Freshly grated Parmigiano-Reggiano cheese, for serving

1. Preheat the oven to 200°F. Line a large rimmed baking sheet with paper towels. Pour enough oil into a large, deep saucepan to come halfway up the sides and heat to 350°F.

2. In a medium mixing bowl, whisk the egg with the water. Add the flour, parsley, and salt and whisk just until combined. The batter should be a little lumpy.

3. In batches, dip the florets into the batter, letting the excess batter drip back into the bowl, and deep-fry until golden brown, about 3 minutes. Do not crowd the cauliflower in the oil. Using a slotted spoon, transfer the cauliflower to the baking sheet and keep warm in the oven while frying the remainder. Let the oil reheat to 350°F between batches.

4. Heap the cauliflower onto a platter, sprinkle with the Parmigiano and the additional parsley, and serve hot.

Fabulicious!

Cotto Calamari Rings

Makes 6 servings

In Italian, *cotto* means "cooked"—which is just a nicer way of saying "fried." No Italian gathering, big or small, is complete without fried calamari. To add a spicy kick to The Quickie Tomato Sauce used for dipping, mix in 1 teaspoon red pepper flakes.

Olive oil, for deep-frying

1½ pounds calamari, cleaned, without tentacles

1 cup all-purpose flour

⅓ cup dry breadcrumbs

½ teaspoon salt

2 cups The Quickie Tomato Sauce (page 22), heated

1. Preheat the oven to 200°F. Line a large rimmed baking sheet with paper towels. Pour enough oil into a large, deep saucepan to come halfway up the sides and heat to 350°F.

2. Cut the calamari crosswise into ¼-inch-thick rings. In a medium mixing bowl, combine the flour, breadcrumbs, and salt; stir to blend.

3. In batches, add the calamari to the flour mixture and toss just to coat. Add the coated calamari to the oil and deep-fry until golden brown, about 2 minutes. Do not crowd the calamari in the oil. Using a slotted spoon, transfer the calamari to the baking sheet and keep warm in the oven while frying the remainder. Let the oil reheat to 350°F between batches.

4. Heap the calamari onto a platter and serve hot, with the sauce on the side for dipping.

---

* * * Girls Who Make Passes . . . * * *

If I can teach you nothing else in this entire book, learn this: flirt with your butcher! He'll not only give you the best cuts, and tell you how to prepare them, but he'll gladly do your dirty work. Don't like to trim the fat? Hate deboning? A pretty smile, and he'll do it for you. Looking for calamari rings? Tell the butcher, and he'll cut them all nice. No nasty tentacles for you. He's a professional. Let him serve you. It will save you tons of time in the kitchen, and maybe even money in the checkout line. Win, win, win.

Fabulicious!

CHAPTER 7

The Main (Meaty) Event

Are you finally ready for dinner? Me, too! What are you making? You're probably waiting for me to tell you, right? Well, I have eight fabulicious dishes right here for you: classic Italian chicken, fish and seafood fantasies, and plenty of beef. (Vegetarians, you might want to flip ahead to the next chapter. I'll hook you up, promise.)

Hunter's Chicken Cacciatore

Makes 4 to 6 servings

Chicken *cacciatore* is a "hunter's" chicken because it uses mushrooms and herbs easily gotten from the forests of central Italy. I add extra veggies to my dish because you can never get enough of them into your kids! The longer you simmer the chicken, the easier it will just fall off the bone. It's a long-cooking dish, but easy and so worth the wait! This would also work great in a slow cooker.

2 tablespoons extra-virgin olive oil

6 skinless chicken thighs on the bone (about 1 1/2 pounds)

10 ounces cremini or white mushrooms, sliced

1 medium onion, chopped

1 red bell pepper, seeded and cut into 1/2-inch dice

2 garlic cloves, minced

1 cup hearty red wine, such as Shiraz

2 cups The Quickie Tomato Sauce (page 22)

2 teaspoons dried oregano

1/2 teaspoon red pepper flakes

1 medium zucchini, cut into 1/2-inch dice

1 tablespoon chopped fresh basil, plus more for garnish

Salt and freshly ground black pepper

Audriana's Creamy Polenta (page 47), for serving (optional)

1. Heat 1 tablespoon of oil in a Dutch oven or flameproof casserole over medium-high heat. Add the chicken and cook, turning occasionally, until browned, about 6 minutes. Transfer chicken to a plate.

2. Add the remaining tablespoon of oil to the Dutch oven and heat over medium heat. Add the mushrooms, onion, red pepper, and garlic. Cook, stirring occasionally, until the vegetables soften, about 6 minutes.

3. Pour in the wine and bring to a boil. Stir in the tomato sauce, oregano, and red pepper flakes. Return the chicken to the Dutch oven, and bring the sauce to a boil. Reduce the heat to medium-low. Simmer for 1 hour. Add the zucchini. Continue cooking until the meat is very tender and pulling away from the bone, about 1 1/4 hours. During the last 10 minutes, stir in the basil.

4. Transfer the chicken to a cutting board. Cut into bite-sized chunks, discarding the skin and bones, and return the meat to the sauce. Season with salt and pepper. Serve hot, over polenta, if you wish, and garnished with a sprinkle of basil.

Roasted Rosmarino Chicken

★ ★ ★ ★ (S) (as long as you don't eat the skin!) **★ ★ ★ ★**

Makes 6 servings

If you've never done it before, roasting a whole chicken can seem intimidating, but it's actually soooo easy and so delicious! The secret is to stuff the bird with things that will steam it from the inside to keep the meat moist. I know touching raw chicken or sticking your hand up a bird isn't everyone's idea of fun, but we're not going to form fancy stuffing balls or anything. Just close your eyes, shove it all in, and know that when it's fully cooked, you will be an official rock star! If you don't want to stick your fingers under the skin, you can certainly skip that step (or call in someone else, smile real pretty, and make them do it).

6 sprigs fresh rosemary

3 tablespoons extra-virgin olive oil

1 lemon, halved

1½ teaspoons salt

1 teaspoon freshly ground
    black pepper

1 (7- to 7½-pound) roasting
    chicken, rinsed and patted dry
    with paper towels

1 small onion, quartered

½ cup dry white wine, such as
    Pinot Grigio

1. Position a rack in the center of the oven and preheat to 375°F.

2. Finely chop the leaves from 2 rosemary sprigs; you should have 1 tablespoon. Discard the stems. Reserve the remaining sprigs. In a large mixing bowl, combine the chopped rosemary, olive oil, the juice of ½ lemon, and the salt and pepper; stir to blend. Reserve the squeezed lemon half.

3. Slide your fingers underneath the skin of the chicken breast to loosen it. Spoon about 1 tablespoon of the rosemary oil under one side of the breast, and massage the skin to distribute the oil as best you can over the breast meat. Repeat on the other side of the breast. Put

---

✳ ✳ ✳ Teresa's Tip ✳ ✳ ✳

It's worth investing in a small meat thermometer to make sure your family's meat is cooked to the right temperature and safe to eat. Most thermometers will tell you right on the dial what temperature each type of meat should be. For chicken, the thermometer should read 170°F when inserted in the thickest part of the bird.

the chicken in the bowl and rub the remaining rosemary oil all over the bird to give it a nice, full-body massage. Shove the onion, both lemon halves, and the reserved rosemary sprigs into the body cavity.

4. Place the chicken on a rack in a metal roasting pan. (Don't have a rack? Twist a long strip of aluminum foil into rope, and shape it into a large ring to fit the pan.) Roast the chicken, basting about every 30 minutes with the pan juices, until it is an amazing golden brown and an instant-read thermometer inserted in the thickest part of the thigh without touching a bone reads 170°F, about 2 1/2 hours.

5. Remove the pan with the chicken from the oven. Tilt the chicken so some of the juices run out of the cavity and into the pan. Transfer the chicken to a carving board and let stand for 10 to 15 minutes, a rest that allows the juices to settle in all the right, yummy places.

6. Pour the pan juices into a glass measuring cup and let stand a few minutes. Skim off and discard the clear yellow fat that rises to the top. Pour the degreased pan juices back into the roasting pan. Place the pan over medium heat and heat until the juices sizzle. Pour in the wine and bring to a boil, scraping up the delicious browned bits in the bottom of the pan. This doesn't make a lot of sauce, but you'll be glad you have it when you taste it.

7. Carve the chicken, discarding the stuff inside. Lay the pieces on the platter and drizzle with the carving juices and sauce. Serve hot.

* * * Juicy Bits from Joe * * *

We always roast a big mother of a chicken so we have leftovers for salads, sandwiches, soups, and midnight snacks. It takes a couple of hours, but there is very little actual work. Do it on a weekend when you have a little extra time.

Devil Shrimp with Angel Hair Pasta

Makes 4 to 6 servings

As you know by now, Joe and I like things spicy (after 11 years of marriage, that's a good thing!). This is one of our favorite meals—great for the entire family or just a romantic dinner. It's an *arrabiata* ("angry") sauce over sweet spaghetti.

2 tablespoons extra-virgin olive oil

1 pound medium (21 to 25 count) shrimp, peeled and deveined

2 garlic cloves, minced

3 cups Snappy Red Sauce (page 22)

1/2 teaspoon red pepper flakes, or more to taste

1/4 teaspoon freshly ground black pepper

1 tablespoon freshly squeezed lemon juice

Salt

1 pound angel hair pasta

1. Bring a large pot of lightly salted water to a boil.

2. Meanwhile, heat 1 tablespoon of oil in a large saucepan over medium-high heat. Add the shrimp and cook, turning once, until it turns opaque, about 3 minutes. Transfer to a plate.

3. Add the remaining tablespoon of oil and the garlic to the saucepan and stir until the garlic is softened but not browned, about 30 seconds. (The pan will be hot, so be careful not to burn the garlic.) Add the tomato sauce, red pepper flakes, and black pepper and bring to a boil. Reduce the heat to medium-low. Return the shrimp to the saucepan and stir in the lemon juice. Cook just to heat the shrimp through, about 1 minute. Season the sauce with salt, and add more red pepper flakes if you want the sauce really devilish. Remove from heat.

4. Meanwhile, add the pasta to the water and cook according to the package directions until al dente. Drain well. Transfer the pasta to individual bowls and top with the shrimp and sauce. Serve hot.

Fabulicious!

113

Little Mermaid's
Baked Flounder Oregano

* * * * S Q * * * *

Makes 6 servings

Everyone in my family loves this simple fish dish of moist flounder fillets with an herb-crumb topping. Folding the fish in half keeps it from getting overdone in the hot oven.

6 (4- to 5-ounce) flounder or
    sole fillets
½ teaspoon salt
¼ teaspoon freshly ground
    black pepper
2 tablespoons dry white wine
1 tablespoon freshly squeezed
    lemon juice
¼ cup dry breadcrumbs
2 tablespoons chopped fresh
    Italian parsley
1 teaspoon dried oregano
2 tablespoons extra-virgin olive oil
Lemon wedges, for serving

1. Position a rack in the top third of the oven and preheat the oven to 400°F. Lightly oil a 13 x 9-inch baking dish.

2. Season the flounder with the salt and pepper. Fold each fillet in half crosswise, tip to tip. Arrange in the baking dish. Drizzle the wine and lemon juice over the fillets.

3. In a small mixing bowl, combine the breadcrumbs, parsley, and oregano. Top each fillet with an equal amount of the breadcrumb mixture. Drizzle with the olive oil.

4. Bake until the fish flakes easily when prodded with the tip of a knife, about 15 minutes. Serve hot, with lemon wedges.

* * * Yes, Yes It Is * * *

A good way to get kids to eat fish is to explain to them that fish are our friends—our good, tasty friends. Remind them of the Little Mermaid's pal, Flounder. We love Flounder! I'm obviously kidding, but it helps to have a sense of humor in the kitchen, especially when faced with stubborn spouses and tantrumming toddlers. I have found that going overboard with the drama actually breaks it up and soon everyone is giggling. "What? You think this is disgusting? It looks like weeds? Oh no, it's not weeds. It's worm guts. Or maybe baby bunny stew. I can't remember . . ."

Fabulicious!

Steak Braciole Roll

Makes 4 servings

A *braciole* is a thin piece of steak marinated and rolled with other ingredients. You can pan-fry it, but I like it baked. It's so easy, but looks and tastes completely gourmet!

¼ cup extra-virgin olive oil

¼ cup balsamic vinegar

2 tablespoons chopped fresh Italian parsley

2 garlic cloves, minced

¼ teaspoon salt

¼ teaspoon freshly ground black pepper

1 (1½ pound) flank steak, butterflied

4 ounces thinly sliced prosciutto

4 ounces sliced provolone cheese

⅓ cup (1½ ounces) freshly grated Pecorino Romano cheese

1 tablespoon chopped fresh basil

1. Combine the oil, vinegar, parsley, garlic, salt, and pepper in a large, resealable plastic bag. Close the bag and shake to mix the ingredients. Add the steak, close the bag, and massage the meat through the bag to coat it on all sides. Refrigerate for at least 2 and up to 12 hours.

2. Position a rack in the center of the oven and preheat the oven to 350°F.

3. Remove the steak from the marinade, letting the excess marinade drip back into the bag. Reserve the marinade. Pat the steak dry with paper towels. Place the steak, with the grain running vertically, on a large piece of aluminum foil to catch any drips.

4. Layer the prosciutto, and then the provolone, over the steak. Sprinkle with the grated cheese, and then the basil. Starting at a long side of the steak, roll up the meat with the grain like a jelly roll. (If you are under 50 years old, think of a Hostess Ho Ho.) Tie kitchen string around the roll every 2 inches or so to keep it from falling apart during cooking.

5. Place the roll (without the foil) in a baking dish just large enough to hold it. Pour the marinade over the top. Bake, basting every 15 minutes with the marinade in the baking dish, until the meat feels tender when pierced with a meat fork, about 1 hour. Remove from the oven and let stand for 15 minutes so all the juices soak back into the meat.

6. Remove the strings. Transfer the roll to a carving board. Holding the knife at an angle, cut the roll crosswise (you will be cutting across the grain now, which will make the tough flank steak more tender) into ½-inch-thick slices. Serve hot, with the marinade from the pan spooned on top.

✳ ✳ ✳ **Butterfly Steak** ✳ ✳ ✳

To butterfly the flank steak, place the steak on the work surface in front of you, with the grain of the meat (it really looks like the grain in wood) running vertically. Using a sharp, thin-bladed knife, starting at a long side of the meat, make a long incision into the center of the steak. Keep cutting, reaching deeper and deeper into the steak, until you are about 1/4 inch from the opposite side. Stop cutting, and open the steak up like a book.

When in Rome . . .	*When in Jersey . . .*
Braciole = brah-CHO-leh	Braciole = bra-ZHOLE

Joe's Juicy Meatballs

Makes 4 to 6 servings

Every self-respecting Italian cook needs a good meatball recipe, and this one is great! Like in life, bigger is better, so these are big, fat, juicy meatballs. With my special sauce of course! Since it's all about the ground beef, get the best stuff you can find: grass-fed, organic, no added hormones.

1 pound ground round (85% lean)

½ cup dry Italian-seasoned breadcrumbs

½ cup milk (preferably 2%)

⅓ cup plus 1 tablespoon freshly grated Pecorino Romano cheese

1 large egg, beaten

3 tablespoons chopped fresh Italian parsley

2 garlic cloves, minced

¾ teaspoon salt

¼ teaspoon freshly ground black pepper

3½ cups Snappy Red Sauce (page 22)

1. Position a rack in the center of the oven and preheat the oven to 400°F. Lightly oil a rimmed baking sheet.

2. In a large mixing bowl, combine the ground round, breadcrumbs, milk, grated cheese, egg, parsley, garlic, salt, and pepper. Knead everything together with clean hands. Feel for the right texture—it should be soft, but not sopping wet, so add a little more milk or breadcrumbs if needed. Form 12 egg-sized balls by gently shaping the meat mixture in your hands. Do NOT crush and mold the meat between your palms! Baby and coax it lovingly into the balls.

3. Place the balls on the baking sheet. Bake until browned, about 30 minutes.

4. Bring the tomato sauce to a boil in a large saucepan. Add the meatballs and return to the boil. Reduce the heat to medium-low. Simmer, stirring occasionally, until the meatballs are cooked through, about 30 minutes. Serve hot.

Calabrian Pork Chops with Peppers and Potatoes

* * * * S * * * *

Makes 4 servings

The Calabria region of Italy is known for spicy dishes. I'll leave it up to you how hot you want to make this dish. You can use sweet peppers, half sweet and half hot, or go all out.

7 tablespoons extra-virgin
   olive oil, divided

2 tablespoons red wine vinegar

2 teaspoons finely chopped
   fresh basil

1 teaspoon dried oregano

2 garlic cloves, minced

½ teaspoon salt

¼ teaspoon freshly ground
   black pepper

4 (6-ounce) boneless pork loin
   chops, cut into 1-inch pieces

1¼ pounds medium red potatoes,
   cut lengthwise into sixths

6 hot or sweet fresh cherry
   peppers, tops removed, seeded
   and quartered

1. In a medium glass or ceramic mixing bowl, whisk 3 tablespoons of the oil with the vinegar, basil, oregano, garlic, salt, and pepper. Let stand for 15 minutes for the ingredients to get to know one another. Add the pork and mix to let it join the party for another 15 minutes.

2. Heat 2 tablespoons of the oil in a large skillet over high heat. Remove the pork from the marinade, letting the excess marinade drip back into the bowl. In batches, add the pork to the skillet and cook, turning occasionally, until the pork is browned, about 4 minutes. Transfer the browned pork to a plate. Leave any remaining fat in the skillet.

3. Add the remaining 2 tablespoons oil to the skillet and reduce the heat to medium. Add the potatoes and peppers and stir well. Cook, stirring often, until the potatoes begin to soften, about 5 minutes. Add ½ cup of water and cover. Cook, stirring occasionally, until the water evaporates and the potatoes are almost tender and lightly browned, about 15 minutes. Return the pork to the skillet; cover and cook until the potatoes are tender, about 5 minutes more. Season with salt and pepper. Serve hot.

* * * Teresa's Tip * * *

If you can't find fresh cherry peppers, you can use pickled cherry peppers, available in jars or at the deli or olive bar sections of the market. These won't need cooking, so just add them to the potatoes with the browned pork.

Stuffed Eggplant with Sausage

Makes 4 servings

This is one of my all-time favorite recipes! I could eat this every single day! It's a bit of work, and—I'm not gonna lie—it's not the prettiest dish, but it's soooo good!

2 medium eggplants (1 to
  1¼ pounds each)
2 tablespoons extra-virgin olive oil
1 medium onion, finely chopped
2 garlic cloves, minced
1 cup fresh breadcrumbs (process
  slightly stale bread with the
  crusts removed in the blender
  or food processor)
½ cup (2 ounces) freshly grated
  Pecorino Romano cheese
4 ounces dry Italian sausage or
  hard salami, chopped into
  small pieces
¼ cup chopped fresh
  Italian parsley
1 large egg, beaten
½ teaspoon salt
¼ teaspoon red pepper flakes
3½ cups The Quickie Tomato
  Sauce (page 22)

1. Position a rack in the center of the oven and preheat the oven to 350°F. Bring a large pot of lightly salted water to a boil over high heat.

2. Trim the eggplants, and slice each one in half lengthwise. Using a paring knife, cut out and discard the visible clusters of seeds (a few seeds left behind in the eggplants won't hurt). Scoop out or cut enough flesh from each half to make a ¼- to ½-inch-thick shell. Preserve the shells, and chop the eggplant flesh into a small dice.

3. Add the eggplant shells to the pot of boiling water and cook, turning occasionally, until softened, about 5 minutes. Carefully drain the eggplants in a colander, rinse under cold water, and let cool.

4. Heat the oil in a large skillet over medium-high heat. Add the diced eggplant and cook, stirring often, until softened, about 4 minutes. Move the eggplant to one side of the skillet. Add the onion and garlic to the empty side of the skillet. Cook until beginning to soften, about 2 minutes. Stir the eggplant, onion, and garlic together and cook until the vegetables are tender, about 2 minutes more. Transfer to a large bowl and let cool slightly. Add the breadcrumbs, grated cheese, sausage, parsley, egg, salt, and red pepper flakes to the eggplant mixture and stir to combine.

5. Pat the eggplant shells dry with paper towels. Season the insides of the shells with salt. Fill each eggplant shell with the eggplant-sausage mixture. Place each eggplant shell on a 12-inch square of aluminum foil, and top with ¼ cup of the tomato sauce. Bring up the edges of the foil and crimp closed. Place the wrapped eggplants on a baking sheet. Bake until the eggplant shells are tender and the filling is heated through, about 30 minutes.

6. Meanwhile, reheat the remaining 2½ cups tomato sauce in a small saucepan over medium heat, about 5 minutes. Transfer to a serving bowl and cover with aluminum foil to keep warm. Unwrap the eggplants and transfer to dinner plates. Serve the eggplants hot, with the tomato sauce passed on the side.

CHAPTER 8

The Wild Side

By now, you've totally rocked a few main courses and are bitchin' in the kitchen. But I don't want you to have to serve Rice-a-Roni or mashed potatoes as a side dish because you didn't have any other recipes. So here is a full chapter of Italian veggie side dishes that are all picky-eater approved.

Me and Joe when we were dating, 1997.

Fontina Potato Torta

Makes 6 servings

This is my Italian twist on scalloped potatoes, and it's not only the most delicious potato dish you'll ever have, it's the prettiest. The trick is to cut the potatoes super thin (a mandoline slicer or plastic V-slicer works much better than just a knife for this) and to pack the potatoes in a small baking dish. After it's cooked, let it sit and settle so it's not watery. To serve, you can scoop sloppy spoonfuls, or cut it into rectangular slices, like lasagna.

2 tablespoons extra-virgin olive oil

1 medium onion, minced

2 garlic cloves, minced

2 pounds baking potatoes, peeled and sliced into ⅛-inch-thick rounds

1 cup canned reduced-sodium chicken broth

1 cup heavy cream

1 teaspoon chopped fresh thyme

Salt and freshly ground black pepper

1 cup (4 ounces) shredded fontina cheese

1. Position a rack in the center of the oven and preheat to 425°F. Lightly oil an 8-inch square baking dish.

2. Heat the oil in a large, wide saucepan over medium heat. Add the onion and cook, stirring often, until the onion softens, about 3 minutes. Stir in the garlic and cook until fragrant, about 1 minute. Add the potatoes and stir well. Add the broth, cream, and thyme and bring to a simmer. Reduce the heat to medium-low. Simmer, gently stirring occasionally, until the potatoes are almost tender and the cream has thickened, about 20 minutes. Season with salt and pepper.

3. Carefully pour the mixture into the baking dish and spread evenly. Sprinkle with the shredded cheese. Place the dish on a baking sheet. Bake until the sauce is bubbling around the edges and the potatoes are tender, about 20 minutes. Let stand for 10 minutes. Serve hot.

✴ ✴ ✴ Juicy Bits from Joe ✴ ✴ ✴

There are a lot of fontina cheeses out there, from the granddaddy and original Fontina Val d'Aosta (one of the best Italian cheeses, but pricey), to domestic kinds and even some from Sweden (who knew?). Use the one that makes you happy and fits your budget, but I have to say my favorite is the Italian Fontina Val d'Aosta. It's just real creamy and has a great earthy flavor that will give your dish a good kick.

Ravishing Broccoli Rabe

★ ★ ★ ★ (S · Q) ★ ★ ★ ★

Makes 4 to 6 servings

If you've never had broccoli rabe before, be prepared: it has a sharp, peppery taste. And of course, I add more peppers to it. But this is for a fancy side dish. You can cook broccoli rabe by itself and season however you wish. After you remove it from the ice water, you can eat it plain or drizzle it with olive oil. If you want to cook out some of the sharpness, boil it longer, but know that it will turn a less-exciting olive color.

1 pound broccoli rabe,
    stems trimmed
1 tablespoon extra-virgin olive oil
1 sweet onion, such as Maui or
    Vidalia, cut into thin half-moons
2 garlic cloves, minced
¼ teaspoon red pepper flakes
Salt
Freshly grated Parmigiano-
    Reggiano cheese, for serving
    (optional)

1. Fill a large bowl halfway with ice water. Set aside.

2. Bring a large pot of lightly salted water to a boil over high heat. Add the broccoli rabe and cook for 2 minutes, no longer, just to set the color. Drain in a colander. Transfer the broccoli rabe to the bowl filled with ice water. Let stand in the ice-water bath until completely cooled, about 10 minutes. Drain again and pat dry with paper towels.

3. Meanwhile, heat the oil in a large skillet over medium heat. Add the onion and cook, stirring occasionally, until golden brown, about 10 minutes. Stir in the garlic and red pepper flakes and stir until the garlic is fragrant, about 1 minute.

4. Add the broccoli rabe and ¼ cup water. Cook, stirring occasionally, until the broccoli rabe is tender and heated through, about 5 minutes. Season with salt. Serve hot, with grated Parmigano sprinkled on top, if you wish.

* * * Meet Broccoli Rabe * * *

Although it's been popular in the Mediterranean for centuries, broccoli rabe—also called rapini, raab, or turnip broccoli—is only just becoming popular in American kitchens. It's not actually broccoli at all. It looks more like cabbage with little broccoli flowers than the tight bunch of broccoli you're used to seeing, but we Italians consider it a much sexier vegetable. And it's packed with nutrients, including the kind believed to zap cancer. One cup of raw broccoli rabe has tons of vitamins C and beta-carotene, a good bit of vitamins A and K, and a whopping 3 grams of protein!

When in Rome . . .

Broccoli rabe = BROCK-oh-lee ROB

* * * Juicy Bits from Joe * * *

When you buy broccoli rabe, look for nice, fresh, dark green leaves. You don't want nothing yellow or wilted. And since you buy it in big bunches, you might as well cook it all up at once. Then once you strain it, you can put the extra in freezer bags and store it there. Next time you need broccoli rabe in a recipe, just take it out of the freezer, throw it in a pan with some olive oil or garlic—and bam, you're done!

Roasted Asparagus alla Parmigiana

★★★★ S Q ★★★★

Makes 4 servings

In Naples, they crumble hard-cooked eggs over the asparagus right before serving. We only eat it that way in the spring, around Easter, when we have a fridge full of (mostly glittery) hard-boiled eggs. Asparagus is one of those things that you should cook to your liking. Some people like it soft. Others—like me—like it to have a little more crunch. The thicker the asparagus stalk you buy, the longer it will take to cook (hint: find thin!).

1 pound thin asparagus, woody stems snapped off
1 tablespoon extra-virgin olive oil
Salt and freshly ground black pepper
2 tablespoons (1½ ounce) freshly grated Parmigiano-Reggiano cheese
1 tablespoon balsamic vinegar

1. Position a rack in the top third of the oven and preheat to 450°F.

2. Spread the asparagus in a single layer on a rimmed baking sheet. Drizzle with the oil. Roll the asparagus in the oil to coat. Season with salt and pepper.

3. Roast, turning the asparagus after 5 minutes, until the asparagus is crisp-tender, about 10 minutes (or longer for more tender asparagus). Immediately transfer to a platter. Sprinkle with the grated Parmigiano, and drizzle with the vinegar. Serve hot.

Fabulicious!

✦ ✦ ✦ **Antonia + Giacinto Gorga** ✦ ✦ ✦

Back in Sala Consilina, I started dating Giacinto when I was 13 years old. He was 19. His father said we needed to date for two years before we got married, but my aunt said, "No, she has no mother. She has no father. She has to get married right away or they no see each other." You didn't just date around back then. You couldn't even talk to a boy in the street. But he didn't even have a house. So we broke up. He went to Capri, then America, but he never forgot me. He even had his father watching me, making sure I was a good girl. Then, after 5 years, he sent me a letter. Said he wanted to get back together. I said, "Come back to Italy, we'll talk." He came back, knocked on my door, and told my grandmother he wanted to marry me. He was very handsome, and I always thought about him. We got married 87 days later.

—Antonia Gorga

Salerno Stuffed Artichokes

Makes 4 servings

Another one of my most favorite dishes in the whole world! These artichokes are often served as starters at holiday dinners, but there's no reason why they can't be a lunch or simple supper main course.

4 large artichokes

1 lemon, halved

2 large eggs, beaten

2 cups fresh breadcrumbs (process slightly stale bread with the crusts removed in the blender or food processor)

4 ounces dry Italian sausage or hard salami, cut into 1/4- to 1/2-inch dice

1/4 cup chopped fresh Italian parsley

1/2 cup (2 ounces) freshly grated Pecorino Romano cheese

1 garlic clove, minced

1/4 teaspoon salt

1/4 teaspoon freshly ground black pepper

2 tablespoons extra-virgin olive oil

1 cup The Quickie Tomato Sauce (page 22)

1. Cut the stems off the artichokes so they sit securely. Trim off and discard 1 inch of leaves from the top of each artichoke. Using kitchen scissors, snip off the thorny tips from the remaining leaves. As you work, rub the cut surfaces with the cut side of the lemon half to keep the artichokes from discoloring too much. (They will turn a little brown no matter what you do.)

2. Beat the eggs in a large mixing bowl. Add the breadcrumbs, sausage, parsley, grated cheese, garlic, salt, and pepper and mix well.

3. Working with one artichoke at a time, using your fingers, pack one-quarter of the stuffing between the outer layers of the tougher leaves, spreading the leaves as best you can. At first, it won't seem like it will all fit, but hang in there, being sure to use all of the crevices between the leaves. Don't bother with the thin leaves that form the artichoke "heart." Press any remaining stuffing over the top of the artichoke.

4. Heat the oil in a large skillet over medium-high heat. Carefully put the artichokes, upside down, into the skillet—be sure the stuffing is well packed so it stays in place. Cook until the stuffing on the top of the artichoke is golden brown, about 2 minutes. Transfer to a plate, right-side up.

5. Combine the tomato sauce and 1 cup water in a Dutch oven or casserole deep enough for the artichokes to sit in, and bring to a boil. Add the artichokes, stuffed-sides up, to the Dutch oven and reduce the heat to medium-low. Cover tightly. Simmer and steam, adding more water to the sauce if it thickens too much and threatens to burn, until a bottom leaf of an artichoke can be pulled off without any resistance, about 1 hour. Transfer each artichoke and some sauce to a shallow soup bowl and serve hot.

∗ ∗ ∗ Teresa's Tip ∗ ∗ ∗

If you can't find dry Italian sausage (or want a substitute), you can use 4 slices of cooked bacon or hard salami in the stuffing instead. Or, if you want to go all veggie, leave out the meat altogether.

Spaghettini with Pesto, Parsley, and Lemon

* * * * **Q** * * * *

Makes 6 side-dish servings

Unlike in America, where pasta is often the main course, in Italy, it's usually just a side. But that doesn't mean it can't be spectacular in its own right. This is great served with grilled chicken or fish.

1 pound spaghettini

1 tablespoon extra-virgin olive oil

3 plum tomatoes, seeded and cut into ½-inch dice

1 cup chopped fresh Italian parsley

½ cup Audriana's Pesto (page 24)

Grated zest of 1 lemon

2 tablespoons freshly squeezed lemon juice

Salt and freshly ground black pepper

1. Bring a large pot of lightly salted water to a boil over high heat. Add the pasta and cook according to the package directions until al dente. Scoop out and reserve ½ cup of the cooking water. Drain the pasta.

2. Meanwhile, heat the oil in a medium skillet over medium-high heat. Add the tomatoes and cook, stirring often, just until heated through, about 2 minutes. Set aside and cover to keep warm.

3. Return the drained pasta to the pot. Add the tomatoes, parsley, pesto, lemon zest, and lemon juice. Toss, adding enough of the reserved cooking water to loosen the pesto and coat the pasta. Season with salt and pepper. Serve hot.

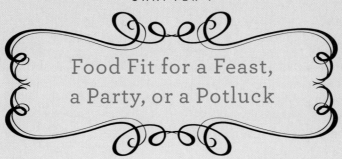

CHAPTER 9

Food Fit for a Feast, a Party, or a Potluck

Whether you're serving a small army at your house, or bringing a dish to a potluck party, it's best if you have everything in one giant pan. Here are my favorite feast recipes. They're easy to make, can be prepared ahead, and will disappear as soon as you serve them up!

Fabulicious!

Real Housewife Rigatoni Bake

Makes 8 to 10 servings

There is nothing better than an Italian pasta bake, especially since you can make it ahead of time and munch on the leftovers (if there are any!) for days. I always make sure to add veggies to my casseroles so my kids are getting more than just meat, pasta, and cheese. To make this casserole completely vegetarian, you can substitute 10 ounces of sliced cremini mushrooms for the sausage.

6 tablespoons extra-virgin olive oil, divided

1 pound sweet Italian pork sausage, casings removed

1 large onion, chopped

1 garlic clove, minced

9 ounces fresh spinach, rinsed but not dried

1 medium eggplant (1 1/4 pounds), cut into 1-inch cubes

3 1/2 cups The Quickie Tomato Sauce (page 22)

Salt

Red pepper flakes

1 pound rigatoni or ziti

1 cup shredded fresh mozzarella cheese (partially freeze for easier shredding)

1. Heat 1 tablespoon of oil in a large nonstick skillet over medium-high heat. Add the sausage and cook, breaking up the meat with the side of a spoon, stirring occasionally, until it loses its raw look, about 6 minutes. Push the sausage to one side of the skillet.

2. Add the onion to the opposite side and cook, stirring the onion occasionally, until translucent, about 4 minutes. Add the garlic, stir the sausage and vegetables together, and cook until the garlic is fragrant, about 1 minute. Transfer to a large bowl.

3. Heat 1 tablespoon of oil in the same skillet over medium-high heat. Add the spinach and cook, stirring occasionally, until the spinach is wilted and tender, about 5 minutes. Drain in a wire sieve. Press on the spinach to extract some of the excess liquid. Stir the spinach into the sausage mixture.

4. Heat 2 tablespoons oil in the skillet over medium-high heat. Add half of the eggplant to the skillet. Cook, stirring occasionally, until the eggplant is lightly browned, about 3 minutes. Do not add more oil to the skillet. Add 1/4 cup water and cover the skillet. Cook until the eggplant is tender and the water has evaporated, about 5 minutes. Add to the sausage mixture. Repeat with the remaining 2 tablespoons oil and eggplant, and another ¼ cup water. Add the eggplant to the sausage mixture, then stir in the tomato sauce. Season with salt and red pepper flakes.

5. Meanwhile, bring a large pot of lightly salted water to a boil over high heat. Add the rigatoni and cook according to the package directions until al dente. Drain well and return to the cooking pot. Add the sausage and vegetable sauce and stir well. Lightly oil a 15 x 10-inch baking dish. Spread the pasta mixture in the baking dish. Sprinkle with the mozzarella. (The pasta can be prepared, cooled, covered, and refrigerated up to 8 hours ahead. Uncover before baking.)

6. Position a rack in the center of the oven and preheat the oven to 350°F. Bake until the sauce is bubbling and the cheese is melted, about 20 minutes. (Allow 30 minutes if the pasta was refrigerated.) Serve hot.

S SKINNY VARIATION:

Make the sauce with Italian turkey sausage. Substitute 1/4 cup freshly grated Parmigiano-Reggiano cheese for the mozzarella.

Crispy, Spicy Chicken Drumsticks

Makes 12 drumsticks

Drumsticks are party-perfect and kid-friendly. And with this recipe, you can cook up a mountain of crisply coated poultry without pulling out a frying pan. The secret is to use crunchy breadcrumbs. I use plain (unseasoned) panko.

1 cup plain yogurt

½ cup milk (whole or skim)

2 garlic cloves, minced

½ teaspoon salt

½ teaspoon red pepper flakes

1¼ cups panko (Japanese-style breadcrumbs)

1 cup (4 ounces) freshly grated Parmigiano-Reggiano cheese

1½ teaspoons dried oregano

1½ teaspoons crumbled dried rosemary

12 skinless chicken drumsticks

3 tablespoons extra-virgin olive oil

1. Position a rack in the top third of the oven and preheat to 375°F. Lightly oil a large, rimmed baking sheet.

2. In a shallow bowl, mix together the yogurt, milk, garlic, salt, and red pepper flakes in a shallow bowl. In a separate shallow bowl, mix together the panko, grated cheese, oregano, and rosemary. Dip each drumstick in the yogurt mixture, letting the excess drip back into the bowl. Add to the panko mixture and turn to coat. Place on the baking sheet. Drizzle with the oil.

3. Bake for 20 minutes. Slip a metal spatula under each drumstick to keep the crust intact, and turn over. Bake until the meat is pulling away from the end of the drumstick, about 45 minutes. Transfer to a platter and serve hot.

Giacinto's Spicy Chicken Scarpariello

Makes 4 to 6 servings

This dish was invented by Italian immigrants who came to America without a lot of money. To save, they would eat meals together, each family bringing something to throw in the pot. They called it *scarpariello,* which means "shoemaker's chicken." No one really remembers why—maybe because it was "cobbled" together? Because even a shoemaker could afford to make it? What makes this dish unique is that it uses chicken and sausage together. What makes it a Gorga-Giudice recipe is all the spiciness!

2 tablespoons extra-virgin olive oil

1 pound hot or sweet Italian pork sausage, with casings, cut into 1-inch chunks

1 pound boneless and skinless chicken breast halves, cut into 1-inch pieces

½ teaspoon salt

½ teaspoon freshly ground black pepper

2 medium red bell peppers, seeded and cut into 1-inch pieces

1 medium onion, chopped

1 to 3 hot red cherry peppers, seeded and minced

2 garlic cloves, minced

½ cup dry white wine

½ cup canned reduced-sodium chicken broth

2 tablespoons balsamic vinegar

½ teaspoon dried oregano

½ teaspoon dried sage

½ teaspoon dried thyme

Chopped fresh Italian parsley, for garnish

Hot cooked orzo, for serving

1. Heat 1 tablespoon of oil in a large skillet over medium heat. Add the sausage and cook, stirring occasionally, until browned, about 5 minutes. Reduce the heat to medium and cook until cooked through, about 5 minutes more. Using a slotted spoon, transfer the sausage to paper towels to drain.

2. Pour off all but 1 tablespoon of the fat from the skillet and return to medium-high heat. Season the chicken with salt and black pepper. Add to the skillet and cook, stirring occasionally, until browned and cooked through, about 10 minutes. Do not overcook the chicken because it will be heated again later. Using the slotted spoon, transfer the chicken to a plate.

3. Add the remaining tablespoon of oil to the skillet and heat over medium heat. Add the red peppers, onion, and hot peppers. Cook, stirring occasionally, until the red peppers are barely tender, about 7 minutes. Stir in the garlic and cook until fragrant, about 1 minute. Add the wine and bring to a boil, stirring up the good scraps in the skillet with a wooden spoon. Stir in the broth and vinegar. Return the sausage and chicken to the pan and sprinkle with the oregano, sage, and thyme. Bring to a boil and cook, stirring often to marry the flavors, for 3 minutes. Season with salt and pepper and sprinkle with the chopped fresh parsley.

4. Serve hot, with the orzo.

S SKINNY VARIATION:

This is just as good with turkey sausage. And if you make it in a nonstick skillet, you can use just 1 teaspoon of oil for browning the sausage and chicken.

My dad with his parents in Sala Consilina, Italy.

Supersize Sausage & Spinach Calzone

Makes 4 servings

We make this all the time for our family, but truth be told, we usually make two of them!

2 tablespoons extra-virgin olive oil, plus more for brushing

2 garlic cloves, thinly sliced

9 ounces fresh spinach, rinsed but not dried

Salt

Red pepper flakes

1 ball Pronto Presto Pizza Dough (page 79)

All-purpose flour, for rolling out the dough

4 ounces dry Italian sausage or hard salami, cut into ¼-inch dice

¼ cup (1 ounce) freshly grated Pecorino Romano cheese

⅓ cup ricotta cheese

1. Position a rack in the center of the oven and preheat to 400°F. Lightly oil a large, rimmed baking sheet.

2. Heat the oil and garlic together in a large skillet over medium heat, stirring often, until the garlic is golden but not browned, about 3 minutes. Add the spinach and cook, stirring often, until just wilted. Do not overcook. Drain in a wire sieve and press on the spinach with a wooden spoon to extract excess moisture. Transfer to a bowl and let cool. Coarsely chop the entire mixture, then season with salt and red pepper flakes.

3. Dust a work surface with flour. Roll, pat, and stretch the dough into a 14-inch round. If it seems stubborn and won't roll, cover the dough with a dry kitchen towel, let it relax for a few minutes, then try again. Transfer the dough to the baking sheet, letting the edges hang over the sides.

4. Stir the chopped sausage into the spinach mixture. Sprinkle the bottom half of the dough with the grated cheese, leaving a 1-inch-wide border at the edge of the round. Spoon the spinach mixture over the grated cheese, then dot with the ricotta. Fold the top half of the dough over to meet the bottom half. Shape the calzone so it fits nicely on the baking sheet. Crimp the edges closed with a fork. Poke a few holes in the top of the calzone with the fork. Brush lightly with oil.

5. Bake until golden brown, about 30 minutes. Let cool for about 5 minutes. Cut into 4 wedges and serve.

Tomato Pizza al Taglio

Makes 8 servings

Pizza *al taglio* means pizza by the slice—square slices cut from a pizza baked in a rectangular pan. Like most Italians, my family are big anchovy eaters (I'd eat them over ice cream—I'm not kidding). But if you like, feel free to substitute sausage or simply omit the anchovies.

5 ripe plum tomatoes

2 tablespoons extra-virgin olive oil

1 garlic clove, minced

½ cup fresh breadcrumbs (process slightly stale bread with the crusts removed in the blender or food processor)

2 medium onions, thinly sliced

2 balls Pronto Presto Pizza Dough (page 79)

All-purpose flour, for rolling out the dough

1 (2-ounce) can anchovy filets, drained and chopped

2 tablespoons pine nuts

2 teaspoons dried oregano

Salt

Red pepper flakes

1. Position a rack in the center of the oven and preheat the oven to 425°F. Lightly oil a half-sheet (18 x 13-inch) pan. Slice the tomatoes crosswise into thin rounds. Shake out the excess seeds, but don't go crazy about it. Place the tomatoes on paper towels to drain.

2. Heat 1 tablespoon of oil and the garlic together in a large skillet over medium heat, stirring often, until the garlic is golden but not browned, about 3 minutes. Add the breadcrumbs and cook, stirring often, until the crumbs are golden brown, about 2 minutes. Transfer to a bowl. Wipe out the skillet with paper towels.

3. Heat the remaining tablespoon of oil in the skillet over medium heat. Add the onions and cook, stirring occasionally, until softened, about 3 minutes. Set aside.

4. Lightly dust a work surface with flour. Roll, stretch, and pat out the dough into an 18 x 13-inch rectangle. Transfer the dough to the half-sheet pan, and stretch to fit the pan. Arrange the tomatoes on the dough, leaving a 1-inch-wide border around the sides. Sprinkle with the onions, anchovies, pine nuts, and oregano, then the breadcrumb mixture.

5. Bake until the crust is golden brown, 20 to 25 minutes. Season with salt and red pepper flakes. Cut into squares and serve hot.

CHAPTER 10

Last (Minute) Suppers

It's no secret—in fact it's frequently televised—that I am usually late getting places. It's not because I mean any disrespect. I actually hate to be late. It's just that I have too much to do! Taking care of four kids, working on all of my businesses, and being a happy wife is no easy task. As you all know. Whether you're a full-time student, single mom, caretaker, hard worker— I know you're as busy as I am! So I'm going to give you my favorite Hail Mary dinners—quick and easy entrées that can be whipped up when you completely forget you have to feed your family.

> ### ✳ ✳ ✳ Freezer-ful ✳ ✳ ✳
>
> There are certain staples you should always have in your freezer (stored in airtight containers) for last-minute dinner emergencies:
>
> * Sausage * Parmigiano-Reggiano cheese
> * Garlic * Breadcrumbs * Vegetables

Vermicelli Pie

★ ★ ★ ★ Q ★ ★ ★ ★

Makes 6 to 8 servings

Vermicelli noodles are slightly thinner than spaghetti; their name is Italian for "little worms." You can substitute spaghetti in this recipe, but it's always fun—especially if you're cooking for boys—to tell them dinner is worm pie. Be sure to use a deep-dish pie plate, or the ingredients won't fit. This is also great with Italian pork or turkey sausage instead of ground beef.

1 tablespoon extra-virgin olive oil

1 medium onion, chopped

1 pound ground beef sirloin (93% lean)

2 garlic cloves, minced

2 cups The Quickie Tomato Sauce (page 22)

½ cup pitted and coarsely chopped Kalamata olives

8 ounces vermicelli or thin spaghetti

2 large eggs, beaten

2 tablespoons unsalted butter, melted

⅓ cup (1½ ounces) freshly grated Parmigiano-Reggiano cheese

¼ teaspoon salt

⅛ teaspoon freshly ground black pepper

1 cup ricotta cheese

½ cup (2 ounces) shredded fresh mozzarella cheese (partially freeze the cheese for easier shredding)

1. Position a rack in the center of the oven and preheat the oven to 350°F. Lightly oil a 9- to 9½-inch (6- to 7-cup capacity) deep-dish pie plate.

2. Heat the oil in a large skillet over medium heat. Add the onion and cook, stirring often, until softened, about 3 minutes. Add the ground sirloin and garlic and cook, stirring often and breaking up the meat with the side of the spoon, until it loses its raw look, about 6 minutes. Add the sauce and olives and bring to a simmer. Reduce the heat to medium-low and cook until the sauce thickens, about 5 minutes.

3. Meanwhile, bring a large pot of lightly salted water to a boil over high heat. Add the vermicelli and cook according to the package directions until al dente. Do not overcook. Drain well in a colander. Transfer to a bowl. Add the beaten eggs and melted butter and mix well. Add the grated Parmigiano, salt, and pepper and mix again.

4. Pour the vermicelli mixture into the pie plate. Spread the mixture with your fingers to form a thick shell, like a piecrust. Spread the ricotta in the bottom of the shell. Top with the tomato sauce.

5. Bake for 20 minutes. Sprinkle with the mozzarella and continue baking until the mozzarella melts, about 5 minutes. Let cool for 5 minutes. Cut into wedges and serve.

✳ ✳ ✳ I Don't Wanna Call You Honey . . . ✳ ✳ ✳

You know you're close with someone when you know their nicknames. So here are ours, Baby Doll. I call my husband "Juicy Joe" because he's so delicious and juicy. ("Joe" is a nickname too; his real name is Giuseppe.) He calls me Tre ("Tree"). My parents call me Tere ("Tah-RAY"). And while I don't have a specific one for each of my girls, I do have tons of pet names I call them all: Baby Doll, of course, Pookie, Gorgeous, Sweetie, and believe it or not, Honey. I really do mean Honey as a term of endearment because I am nice like that.

When in Rome . . .

Vermicelli = ver-mih-CHELL-ee

✳ ✳ ✳ Juicy Bits from Joe ✳ ✳ ✳

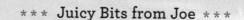

Not a lot of people know this, but I've been making my own wine for years. Me and my father, we started making wine as a tradition when I was a kid. Now Gabriella helps me. All the girls help out, but Gabriella loves it. She comes in, cleans the bottles for me. She's a great helper.

To make your own wine, you need a good wine room. It's the first room I built in my house. If you have a good temperature controlled room with the right stuff, you don't need to put sulfites in your wine, and that's good because it's the sulfites that give you the headaches.

You need grapes of course. You can get whatever type you like. I do Chilean grapes, California grapes, and Italian grapes. I mix it all up. It's hit and miss. Sometimes it's incredible and sometimes it's just OK. It's a little gamble you take. But if you use good grapes, more than likely it's all gonna come out good.

So you take your grapes and you de-stem them and crush them and let them ferment in a tub for about three or four weeks. Then you press it in the wine press, put the juice back in the tub, and let it sit, and ferment. You have to keep passing the wine back and forth into different tubs actually so the sediment sits at the bottom, then you can put it in oak barrels. The longer you leave the wine in the tub though, the darker it will be. I like the darker color, the deep red wine color.

The whole process takes about a year. I probably do about 350 cases a year. My dad, he does about 250 cases. My friends come over and help me out and then of course, we drink it.

Me and Tre are hoping to start a new restaurant in Parsippany, New Jersey called Villa di Vino. It's going to feature all of her great recipes and my wine. When it opens, come by and we'll hook you up!

Pookie's Pesce Primavera

Makes 4 servings

Nothing is faster, tastier, or healthier than baked fish and veggies. You can use any combination of vegetables that you like for this. Look at it as a way to use up some of the produce hanging around in your fridge, but remember that the veggies have to be tasty and fresh.

2 tablespoons extra-virgin olive oil

2 garlic cloves, minced

8 ounces white mushrooms, sliced (about 2 1/2 cups)

3 cups broccoli florets or 1 1/2 cups each broccoli and cauliflower florets

2 large carrots, cut into thin matchsticks

1 celery rib, cut into 1/2-inch-thick slices

1/2 teaspoon salt

1/4 teaspoon freshly ground black pepper

4 tilapia fillets

2 tablespoons freshly squeezed lemon juice

1/4 cup (1 ounce) freshly grated Parmigiano-Reggiano cheese

2 tablespoons chopped fresh basil

1. Position a rack in the center of the oven and preheat to 450°F. Lightly oil a 13 x 9-inch baking dish.

2. Heat 1 tablespoon of oil and the garlic together in a large skillet over medium heat, stirring often, until the garlic is softened but not browned, about 1 minute. Add the mushrooms and cook, stirring often, until they begin to soften, about 2 minutes. Add the broccoli, carrots, and celery and stir well. Add 1/4 cup water and cover. Cook, stirring often, until the vegetables are crisp-tender, about 3 minutes. Season with salt and pepper.

3. Meanwhile, season the tilapia with the salt and pepper. Arrange in the prepared baking dish. Drizzle with the lemon juice, and then the remaining tablespoon of oil. Bake for 5 minutes.

4. Remove the baking dish from the oven. Heap the vegetable mixture over the fish and sprinkle with the grated cheese. Return to the oven and bake until the fish looks opaque when flaked with the tip of a knife, about 10 minutes. Sprinkle with the basil and serve hot.

Fabulicious!

Butterfly Basil Chicken

★ ★ ★ ★ Q ★ ★ ★ ★

Makes 4 servings

Farfalle means "butterfly" in Italian, and my kids just love eating the little bow tie–shaped pasta. This is one of our favorite weeknight meals.

4 tablespoons extra-virgin
olive oil, divided

1 tablespoon balsamic vinegar

1 tablespoon freshly squeezed
lemon juice

1 tablespoon salt

½ teaspoon freshly ground
black pepper

4 (6-ounce) boneless and
skinless chicken breast halves

3 tablespoons finely chopped
fresh basil

2 medium zucchini, cut into
⅛-inch-thick rounds

8 ounces farfalline (tiny
bow-shaped pasta) or farfalle

Chopped fresh Italian parsley
for garnish

1. Bring a large pot of lightly salted water to a boil over high heat. In a small bowl, whisk together 2 tablespoons of oil, the balsamic vinegar, and the lemon juice. Season with salt and pepper and set aside.

2. One at a time, place half a chicken breast between two plastic storage bags. Pound with the flat side of a meat pounder or a rolling pin until the meat is about ½-inch thick. Season the chicken with salt and pepper. Sprinkle on both sides with the chopped basil.

3. Heat 1 tablespoon of oil in a large skillet over medium-high heat. Add the chicken and cook, turning occasionally, until browned on both sides and the chicken feels firm when pressed in the center, 10 to 12 minutes. Transfer to a plate, tent with aluminum foil, and keep warm.

4. Add the remaining tablespoon of oil to the skillet and heat over high heat. Add the zucchini and cook, stirring occasionally, until crisp-tender, about 3 minutes. Season with salt and pepper. Remove from the heat.

5. Meanwhile, add the pasta to the boiling water and cook according to the package directions until al dente. Drain well.

6. Divide the pasta among 4 deep soup bowls. Top each with a chicken breast half, and then equal amounts of the zucchini. Drizzle each serving with the balsamic vinegar mixture. Sprinkle with the parsley and serve.

Bella Sausage and Veggie Bake

Makes 4 to 6 servings

This recipe is extremely flexible, easy to throw together with whatever you have lying around the kitchen (and hopefully, in your freezer). It's also pretty laid back—you toss a few things in the oven, let them cook, add a few more, come back later . . . and eventually you have a beautiful sausage-and-vegetable dinner.

2 large russet potatoes, peeled and cut into 1-inch cubes

2 carrots, cut into ½-inch rounds

3 tablespoons extra-virgin olive oil, divided

1 pound Italian sweet or hot turkey sausage, with casings, cut into 1-inch chunks

3 medium zucchini, cut into ½-inch pieces

1 large red bell pepper, seeded and cut into ½-inch pieces

Salt and freshly ground black pepper

1 cup fresh breadcrumbs (process slightly stale bread with the crusts removed in the blender or food processor)

½ cup (2 ounces) freshly grated Parmigiano-Reggiano cheese

1 garlic clove, minced

1 teaspoon dried oregano

2 tablespoons chopped fresh basil or Italian parsley (optional)

1. Position a rack in the center of the oven and preheat the oven to 425°F. Lightly oil an 18 x 13-inch half-sheet pan.

2. In a mixing bowl, toss together the potatoes, carrots, and 1 tablespoon of oil. Spread in the half-sheet pan. Bake for 15 minutes.

3. In the same bowl, toss together the sausage, zucchini, red pepper, and 1 tablespoon of oil in the bowl. Add to the half-sheet pan with the potatoes and carrots and bake for 30 minutes, until the potatoes are almost tender. Season the sausage and vegetable mixture with salt and pepper.

4. In a medium bowl, mix together the breadcrumbs, grated cheese, garlic, oregano, and remaining table-spoon oil. Sprinkle over the sausage and vegetables. Bake until the crumbs are toasted and the potatoes are tender, about 10 minutes. Sprinkle with the basil, if desired, and serve hot.

Giuseppe's Cheesy Chicken Bucatini

★ ★ ★ ★ **S Q** ★ ★ ★ ★

Makes 4 servings

I love, love, love bucatini! They are thick, but hollow, spaghetti noodles that suck up all the sauce inside so you get super-squishy, juicy bites. *Buco* means "hole" in Italian. Do whatever you want with that knowledge.

2 tablespoons extra-virgin olive oil

1 1/2 pounds boneless and skinless chicken breast halves, cut into 1-inch pieces

1 teaspoon salt

1/2 teaspoon freshly ground black pepper

1 pound bucatini or perciatelli

2 garlic cloves, minced

1/2 cup dry white wine, such as Pinot Grigio

2 tablespoons freshly squeezed lemon juice

1/2 cup (2 ounces) freshly grated Parmigiano-Reggiano cheese, plus more for serving

3 tablespoons chopped fresh basil

3 tablespoons chopped fresh Italian parsley

2 tablespoons unsalted butter

1. Bring a large pot of lightly salted water to a boil over high heat.

2. Heat 1 tablespoon of oil in a large skillet over medium-high heat. Season the chicken with 1 teaspoon salt and 1/2 teaspoon freshly ground pepper. Add to the skillet and cook, stirring occasionally, until browned on all sides and cooked through, about 6 minutes. Transfer to a plate. Set aside.

3. Add the bucatini to the water and cook according to the package directions until al dente. Meanwhile, heat the remaining tablespoon of oil and the garlic together in the same skillet, stirring often, until the garlic is softened but not browned, about 2 minutes. Add the wine and lemon juice and cook, stirring up the browned bits in the skillet with a wooden spoon. Add the chicken and any juices from the plate and stir to reheat the chicken, about 1 minute. Remove from the heat.

4. Drain the bucatini in a colander. Return to the pot. Add the chicken mixture, the grated cheese, basil, parsley, and butter and mix well until the butter melts. Season with more salt and pepper, if you like. Serve hot, with additional grated Parmigiano passed on the side.

* * * **Teresa's Tip** * * *

You can easily substitute shrimp for the chicken in this recipe. Just skip Step 2 and simmer shrimp in the sauce until it is thoroughly cooked.

Fabulicious!

CHAPTER 11

A Happy Ending

You didn't think I'd leave you without a happy ending, did you? Here are some of my family's favorite desserts. They're not all skinny, of course—although some are! (And as promised, none of them use vegetable oil!) I believe as long as you treat your body right, feed it healthy food, and don't eat Olive Garden-sized portions, you can certainly splurge once in awhile. As my mama always says, "Life is short, pass the cannoli!"

✳ ✳ ✳ Vegetable Oil Vendetta ✳ ✳ ✳

It might seem like I have a huge problem with vegetable oil when there are much bigger food villains out there—trans fat, high-fructose corn syrup, partially hydrogenated anything—but you gotta pick your battles, and I do have a thing for olive oil. All oil, no matter if it comes from an olive or a genetically created "canola," contains the same 14 grams of fat per tablespoon, but olive oil is the only oil that is actually a fruit juice. The good stuff—extra-virgin—isn't chemically treated or messed with. If you can only make one huge healthy change in your diet, substitute olive oil for veggie oil whenever you can. And especially when baking, try to avoid oil, period. That's what I do in my family, anyway, so that's why you won't see any vegetable oil in these recipes.

Holy Cannoli Cupcakes

Makes 12 cupcakes

Oh, do I love cannoli, but the shells can be a huge pain to make. They take so long, they have to be just right, and when they break, it's game over. So one day when my girls and I were baking cupcakes (for Milania to take to school for her birthday), we decided to make a cannoli cupcake. It's really a regular cupcake, filled with cannoli cream, and then topped with a special chocolate frosting.

I'm proud of my homemade cupcake recipe for 3 reasons: there's no vegetable oil in it, it's fairly light (½ cup yogurt and ½ cup butter instead of the traditional 1 cup of butter), and you can whip up the batter in a snap in a single bowl. All the dry ingredients get mixed together and then all the wet ones get added in.

Cupcakes

1½ cups all-purpose flour

1 cup granulated sugar

1½ teaspoons baking powder

¼ teaspoon salt

8 tablespoons (1 stick)
   unsalted butter, cubed,
   at room temperature

½ cup lowfat plain yogurt

1 large egg plus 2 large egg
   yolks, at room temperature

1 teaspoon vanilla extract

**(ingredients continued
   on page 168)**

1. Position a rack in the center of the oven and preheat the oven to 350°F. Have your littlest helper put paper liners in a standard 12-cup muffin pan.

2. To make the cupcakes: In a medium mixing bowl, whisk together the flour, sugar, baking powder, and salt. Add the butter, yogurt, egg and yolks, and vanilla. Mix with an electric mixer on medium speed for 3 minutes (set a timer), occasionally scraping down the sides of the bowl with a rubber spatula. Divide the batter evenly among the cups.

3. Bake until the cupcakes are golden brown and a wooden toothpick inserted in the center of a cupcake comes out clean, 20 to 25 minutes. Cool in the pan for 5 minutes.

* * * Teresa's Tip * * *

If you really miss the crunch of the shell, you can roll out a premade piecrust, cut out little circles, dust them in sugar, and bake them. Then stick them on top of your cupcakes for a yummy "spoon."

Cannoli Cream

1 cup ricotta impastata (see
  Juicy Bits from Joe, page 168)
¼ cup confectioners' sugar
½ teaspoon vanilla extract
¼ cup mini chocolate chips

Cocoa Whipped Cream

1⅔ cups heavy cream
¼ cup confectioners' sugar
1 tablespoon unsweetened
  cocoa powder
¼ cup mini chocolate chips,
  for decoration (optional)

Remove the cupcakes from the pan, transfer to a wire cooling rack, and let cool completely.

4. To make the cannoli cream: In a mixing bowl, whisk together the ricotta, confectioners' sugar, and vanilla until smooth. Stir in the mini chocolate chips. Transfer to a quart-sized resealable plastic bag. Using scissors, snip off ½ inch from a closed corner of the bag. You will use the plastic bag as a pastry bag to fill the cupcakes.

5. Using a small knife, cut a deep, inverted cone out of the center of each cupcake, and remove the cones. You won't need the cupcake cones, but I'm sure you can find a willing customer to help you eat them. Use the plastic bag to fill the cupcakes with the cream. Use a knife to smooth the top of the filling flush with the cupcake.

6. To make the cocoa whipped cream: In a chilled medium bowl combine the heavy cream, confectioners' sugar, and cocoa powder and beat with an electric mixer on high speed until the cream forms stiff peaks.

7. Snip ½ inch from a closed corner of a gallon-sized resealable plastic bag. Insert a large star tip (such as Ateco 825) in the bag and poke it through the snipped end. Transfer the cocoa cream to the bag. Pipe swirls of the cocoa whipped cream over each cupcake. If you want, sprinkle each with about 1 teaspoon of mini chocolate chips. Refrigerate, uncovered, until ready to serve.

✱✱✱ Juicy Bits from Joe ✱✱✱

The key to delicious cannoli cream is using the right ricotta—ricotta *impastata*. It's a ricotta that's already been drained so it's very thick and creamy. It's definitely worth looking for at your local Italian deli. They even sell it at the Costco near us. You can use regular ricotta, but you gotta drain it first. There are a couple of ways to do this. The quick way is to wrap the ricotta in cheesecloth and wring it out. The long way is to put paper towels in a sieve, fill it with your ricotta, hang it over a bowl, and then let it sit in the refrigerator overnight.

Happy to See Me Chocolate Salami

Makes 12 to 16 servings

Chocolate salami is a traditional Tuscan fudge-like dessert that's easy to make, doesn't require baking, and looks so pretty when it's sliced and arranged on a plate. However, it does involve using raw eggs. Since I have a no-raw-egg rule in my house—too many babies and old people around (and you know I respect the elderly . . .)—I came up with my own version. It's got the same wonderful texture and chocolaty taste, but with less calories than the traditional four-eggs-and-huge-chunks-of-butter version.

3 cups semisweet chocolate chips

1 (14-ounce) can nonfat sweetened condensed milk

3 cups coarsely crushed dry cookies, such as tea biscuits, vanilla wafers, or animal crackers (they should be about the size of your fingernail, minus the nail extensions)

1½ teaspoons vanilla extract

2 tablespoons confectioners' sugar

1. Combine the chocolate chips and condensed milk in a large microwave-safe bowl. Microwave on medium (50% power), stirring at 1-minute intervals, until the chocolate is melted.

2. Stir in the cookies and vanilla. Let stand until the mixture is firm enough to shape, about 10 minutes.

3. Place a 20-inch-long piece of waxed paper on a work surface. Sift the confectioners' sugar over the waxed paper. Transfer the chocolate mixture to the waxed paper. Shape the chocolate mixture into a thick, 12-inch-log about 1 inch from the bottom of the wax paper. Tightly roll up the log in the waxed paper, and twist and scrunch the ends closed to make a salami shape.

4. Refrigerate until the salami is firm enough to slice, 2 to 3 hours. To serve, let stand for about 30 minutes at room temperature to soften slightly. Remove the waxed paper and slice diagonally.

Fabulicious!

Pretty Pizzelle "Ice Cream" Sandwiches

Makes 6 servings

We do make our own pizzelle cookies for special occasions, but they require a special cooking iron (kinda like a waffle iron) that not everyone has at home. But since a lot of grocery stores now carry delicious premade pizzelle cookies (you can also find them online), and since my kids think every night is a special occasion, we started making these pretty pizzelle cookie sandwiches. Here's the catch: while they are super-easy to make—and great fun for kids—they do have to harden in the freezer for one to two hours before you can eat them. This makes them the perfect dinner bribe. On a night when you're serving a healthy dinner they might normally resist, make this dessert with them first. They'll clean their plates for the pizzelle prize, I promise!

12 vanilla-flavored pizzelle cookies

2 cups lowfat vanilla frozen yogurt, slightly softened at room temperature

½ cup mini chocolate chips or rainbow sprinkles

1. For each sandwich, using a small ice cream scoop or a soupspoon, scoop 4 small balls of frozen yogurt (about ⅓ cup) onto a pizzelle cookie. Carefully spread the frozen yogurt to just beyond the edges of the cookie. Top with a second cookie to make a sandwich.

2. Put the mini chocolate chips in a shallow bowl. Roll the edges of each sandwich in the chips, pressing them to adhere to the frozen yogurt. Place on a baking sheet or large platter. Freeze until the frozen yogurt is frozen again, 1 to 2 hours. Serve frozen.

✳ ✳ ✳ **Designer Logos on Dessert** ✳ ✳ ✳

Pizzelle are Italian wafer cookies that have been eaten—and given as gifts—at holidays for centuries. Each family or village had its own iron crest or special design they would imprint into the cookie before baking it. Delicious, personalized calling-card cookies! What could be better than that? Most electric pizzelle irons today make round cookies, but mine makes heart-shaped ones.

When in Rome . . .

Pizzelle = peet-ZELL-ay

* * * **Teresa's Tip** * * *

Make sure you use vanilla-flavored pizzelles. The standard pizzelle cookie is anise, or licorice-flavored, not the most popular taste for tiny ones.

Confetti Party Cookies

Makes about 40 cookies

These are classic Italian celebration cookies. Every family has their own special recipe. You can squeeze the dough out of a cookie press so it has ridges, or roll it with your hands. The important thing is to form it in the S-shape, and to use the multicolored nonpareil sprinkles (the little balls). Not jimmies, not colored sugar—it has to be the nonpareils!

If you've never had an Italian cookie, and eat one right out of the oven, it may seem a little plain. But put the icing on and some sprinkles, and it's a party in your mouth.

Cookies
3 cups all-purpose flour
1 tablespoon baking powder
¼ teaspoon salt
8 tablespoons (1 stick) unsalted
    butter, at room temperature
½ cup granulated sugar
3 large eggs, beaten
1½ teaspoons vanilla extract

Icing
1 cup confectioners' sugar
2 tablespoons whole or lowfat milk
½ teaspoon vanilla extract
Colored nonpareil sprinkles,
    for decoration

1. Position racks in the top third and center of the oven and preheat the oven to 350°F. Lightly butter 2 large baking sheets, or line them with parchment paper.

2. To make the cookies: Sift together the flour, baking powder, and salt. In a large mixing bowl, combine the butter and sugar and beat with an electric mixer on high speed until pale yellow and light in texture, about 3 minutes. Gradually beat in the eggs, then add the vanilla. Using a sturdy wooden spoon, gradually stir in the flour mixture to make a shaggy dough. Switch to your hands and squish and mix the dough until it comes together. Turn the dough out onto a lightly floured work surface and knead until smooth, about 2 minutes. Cover the dough with a dry towel and let stand for 10 minutes.

3. Roll the dough into 40 walnut-sized balls. One at a time, roll each ball on the work surface underneath your

✳ ✳ ✳ Teresa's Tip ✳ ✳ ✳

This is a great sweet treat to make when you have a lot of people around because it makes A LOT of cookies! (And it's rich, so you really don't need to serve big pieces.)

palms to make a 7½-inch-long rope about ½-inch thick. Roll each end towards the middle, with one curve facing up and the other facing down, to make an "S" shape. Transfer to the baking sheets, spacing the cookies about 1 inch apart.

4. Bake, switching the position of the baking sheets from top to bottom and back to front halfway through baking, until the cookies are set and light brown on the bottoms (pick one up to check), 15 to 20 minutes. Do not overbake. Let cool on the baking sheets for 5 minutes. Transfer to a wire cooling rack and cool completely.

5. To make the icing: Sift the confectioners' sugar into a bowl. Add the milk and vanilla and whisk until smooth.

6. Place the cookies on the rack over a baking sheet. Spoon the icing over the cookies, letting the excess icing drip onto the baking sheet. Immediately scatter the sprinkles over the cookies and let dry. (The cookies will keep in an airtight container for up to a week.)

Franco and Filomena on their wedding day, 1969.

✳✳✳ **Juicy Bits from Joe** ✳✳✳

I guess Tre already told you about her family, so let me tell you a bit about mine. I have one brother, Pietro, and one sister, Maria. They each have three kids. So including Tre's brother's kids, we have nine nieces and nephews total. All good kids. Cute kids. My father's name is Franco. My mother is Filomena. They've been married 42 years. They live real close, and we see them all the time.

San Giuseppe Zeppole

Makes about 18

Zeppole are fried dough balls traditionally associated with San Giuseppe's feast day on March 19. San Giuseppe is Saint Joseph, Jesus' foster father. It's also Father's Day in Italy. Like a lot of Italian classics, every village and every family has its own recipe. Some are sweet, some are rich, and some—like my family's—are very simple.

1 (2 1/4-ounce) envelope instant or
   quick-rising yeast
2 1/2 cups unbleached all-purpose
   flour, as needed
1/4 teaspoon salt
Olive oil, for deep-frying
Confectioners' sugar, for garnish

1. Pour 1 cup cold tap water into a bowl and add the yeast. Stir in 1 cup of the flour and the salt. Gradually stir in enough of the remaining flour to make a soft, sticky dough. Knead the dough in the bowl, adding a little more flour if needed to keep the dough from sticking to your hands, until smooth and elastic, about 5 minutes. Do not add too much flour—the dough is supposed to be moist and tacky.

2. Shape the dough into a ball and let it sit in the bowl. Coat the top of the dough with olive oil. Cover with a damp kitchen towel or plastic wrap. Let stand in a warm, draft-free place until doubled in volume, about 1 hour.

3. Pour enough olive oil into a large, deep saucepan to come halfway up the sides and heat to 350°F. Lay a brown paper bag on a large baking sheet. Rinse your hands under cold water. Working in 2 or 3 batches, pull off golf-ball-sized pieces of dough, shape loosely into balls, and carefully drop into the oil. Fry until the balls puff and turn a beautiful golden brown, 4 to 5 minutes. Using a slotted spoon, remove from the oil and place on the paper bag to drain.

4. Transfer the warm zeppole to a platter. Sift a generous amount of confectioners' sugar through a wire sieve over them. Serve warm.

✳ ✳ ✳ Just Don't Call Them Donut Holes ✳ ✳ ✳

Depending on where you're from—in Italy and in America—you might call *zeppole* (*zeppola* is the singular) by another name: zeppoli, zippuli, sfinge, crispellis, or mangonillis. Some use a potato dough. Some are stuffed with anchovies. But made any way, they are delish!

Stuff It

Instead of dusting the zeppole with confectioner's sugar on the outside, you can flavor zeppole from the inside. Before frying, pull the dough ball apart, stick a piece of apple inside, and close it up. (For a savory appetizer, you could use a piece of anchovy.) Or, after the balls are fried, poke a hole in each one and pipe in Nutella.

Deep-Fried Dilemma

I know, I know, deep-frying anything isn't healthy, and using olive oil to do it isn't cheap. My answer to the health issue is, you should only deep-fry things for very special-occasion treats, and when you do, don't stuff your face. As for the cost, well, in Italy, most cooks can use as much olive oil as they want because it's usually free, crushed from olives right in their backyard! If olives don't grow in your backyard, but you can afford it, I'd still deep-fry with a good extra-virgin olive oil. Even using 3 inches in a pan, it's not going to cost you more than $10, and this is a special dessert we're making. If you want to use a cheaper oil, I'd say go with a regular, non-virgin olive oil. If you have to use a vegetable oil, just don't tell me about it, and we'll pretend this whole thing never happened.

Antonia's Tuscan Apple Torta

Makes 12 servings

This is a fairly hearty, heavy cake in texture, although it's amazingly healthy for a dessert (no butter, no vegetable oil, and just ⅓ egg per serving!). It's not as sweet or airy as a regular bakery cake, but it's not supposed to be. It's more of a pound cake, less of a slather-it-with-frosting cake. Serve in small slices with a little whipped cream or ice cream on the side. You will need an angel food cake pan to bake this—the kind with a tube in the middle and a removable bottom.

5 large eggs, at room temperature

1⅓ cups sugar

1 cup unsweetened, natural
   applesauce

⅓ cup fresh orange juice

2 tablespoons vanilla extract

¼ teaspoon salt

2⅓ cups all-purpose flour

4 teaspoons baking powder

2 Golden Delicious apples

Cinnamon and sugar, for coating
   the apples

1. Preheat the oven to 350°F.

2. In a large mixing bowl, combine the eggs and the sugar and beat with an electric mixer on high speed until they are light and fluffy, at least 3 minutes. Add the applesauce, orange juice, vanilla, and salt, and mix again until just blended.

3. In a separate bowl, sift together the flour and the baking powder. Do not skip the sifting! It's very important! Stir the dry mixture into the wet mixture ½ cup at a time.

4. Peel and core the apples, and then cut them into quarters. Cut each quarter into thin slices ¼-inch thick. (Do not do this ahead of time, as the apple slices will turn brown!) Put half of the apples slices in a bowl and coat with cinnamon and sugar. Leave the other half plain.

5. Grease (really grease!) the pan, even the inside tube. Pour half of the batter in the pan. Lay the sugared apple slices in a single layer on the batter. Pour the remaining batter over the apple slices in the pan.

6. Carefully lay the plain apple slices on top of the cake in a spiral pattern, overlapping each other halfway. If they sink a bit, that's OK. Bake for 45 minutes until golden brown. Set on a wire cooling rack to cool for 5 minutes. Run a knife around the inside of the pan and the tube. Carefully remove the cake from the pan, but leave it on the tube insert. Let cool completely on the wire rack. When cooled, slip a knife between the cake and the insert, and carefully lift up and remove the cake. Transfer the cake to a platter, with the apples on top. Serve with whipped or iced cream and coffee.

Me, my mommy, and Milania in Naples, 2010.

Chocolate Zabaglione Cakelets

Makes 8 servings

This is a super-classy, restaurant-style dessert that you can make at home without a pastry chef degree. Even better, you can whip up the cake in two minutes with ingredients you have on hand, and it doesn't use vegetable oil!

Zabaglione Cream

3 large egg yolks

1/2 cup granulated sugar

2 tablespoons all-purpose flour

1/2 cup sweet Marsala wine

1 1/2 cups heavy cream

Cake

1 cup all-purpose flour

1 cup granulated sugar

3 tablespoons unsweetened
    cocoa powder

1 1/2 teaspoons baking powder

1/2 teaspoon salt

1 cup milk (whole or skim)

8 tablespoons (1 stick) unsalted
    butter, melted

2 large eggs

1 teaspoon vanilla extract

3 cups assorted berries,
    such as raspberries and sliced
    strawberries

Confectioners' sugar, for garnish

1. To make the zabaglione cream: In a medium saucepan, whisk the eggs until they are pale yellow. Gradually whisk in the sugar and whisk until thickened. Whisk in the flour, and then the Marsala. Whisk constantly over medium-low heat until the mixture is thick and is just beginning to bubble, about 5 minutes. Immediately transfer to a medium bowl. Press a piece of plastic wrap directly on the surface of the egg mixture and poke a few holes in the top with a knife. Refrigerate until chilled, at least 2 hours.

2. To make the cake: Position a rack in the center of the oven and preheat to 350°F. Lightly butter a 13 x 9-inch rimmed baking sheet or a baking pan. Line the bottom of the baking sheet with waxed paper (the butter will hold the waxed paper in place.)

3. Sift the flour, sugar, cocoa, baking powder, and salt together into a medium mixing bowl. Add the milk, melted butter, eggs, and vanilla. Mix with an electric mixer on medium speed for 2 minutes (set a timer), occasionally scraping down the sides of the bowl with a rubber spatula. Spread the batter in the baking sheet.

4. Bake until the cake springs back when pressed in the center and it is starting to pull away from the sides, about 20 minutes. Transfer the cake in its pan to a wire cooling rack and let cool completely in the pan.

5. To finish the zabaglione cream: In a chilled medium bowl, whip the heavy cream with an electric mixer on high speed until soft peaks form. Stir about ¼ of the whipped cream into the bowl of the cooled egg mixture to lighten it. Fold in the remaining whipped cream. Refrigerate until ready to serve.

6. To assemble the cakelets: Using a 3-inch diameter drinking glass with straight sides, or a cookie cutter, cut out 8 rounds from the sheet cake. (Nibble on the scraps, or give them as treats to the kids.) For each serving, spoon about ⅓ cup of the zabaglione cream onto a dessert plate. Lean a chocolate round against the cream, and scatter the fruit around it. Sift the confectioners' sugar through a wire sieve over each cakelet and serve immediately.

✳ ✳ ✳ Z-Cream ✳ ✳ ✳

Zabaglione, which literally means "egg punch" in Italian, is a creamy dessert made of whipped egg yolks, sugar, and Marsala wine. It's another dessert-of-a-million-names-and-spellings, including: zabaione, zablaiogne, zabajone, and sabayon.

When in Rome . . .

Zabaglione = zah-bah-YOH-nay

Filomena's Ti Amo Tiramisù

Makes 8 to 12 servings

I love my mother-in-law. I've known her since I was born, and we've always gotten along. That doesn't mean, however, she was gonna give up her secret tiramisù recipe easily. But I showed her all the wonderful letters and requests I got for traditional Italian desserts, and she relented. So here you go . . . for the first time anywhere: Filomena's Ti Amo Tiramisù: the dessert that loves you back.

1½ cups brewed hot
   dark-roast coffee
3 tablespoons orange-flavored
   liqueur, such as Grand Marnier
½ cup plus 1 tablespoon granulated
   sugar, divided
5 large egg yolks
1¼ cups heavy cream, divided
1 (16-ounce) container
   mascarpone cheese
About 40 Italian savoiardi biscuits
   (ladyfingers)
2 tablespoons unsweetened
   cocoa powder
Semisweet chocolate bar,
   for shavings

1. In a shallow bowl, combine the coffee, liqueur, and 1 tablespoon of sugar and stir to dissolve the sugar. Let cool.

2. In the top insert of a double boiler, whisk together the egg yolks, remaining ½ cup sugar, and 2 tablespoons of the heavy cream. Bring an inch of water in the saucepan of the double boiler to a simmer over medium heat; reduce the heat to medium-low. (You can also make your own double boiler set-up with a stainless steel bowl that fits snugly over a medium saucepan; do not allow the bowl to touch the water.) Place the insert over the simmering water. Stir constantly with a rubber spatula, scraping any splashes of the egg mixture off the sides of the insert, until the mixture is thick enough to coat the spatula (if you run your finger through the mixture it will cut a swath) and an instant-read thermometer inserted into the mixture reads 185°F, about 5 minutes.

3. Remove the insert from the double boiler. Immediately whisk the mascarpone into the warm egg mixture, and mix until smooth.

Fabulicious!

4. In a chilled medium bowl, whip the remaining heavy cream with an electric mixer on high speed until soft peaks form. Add the mascarpone mixture and fold together.

5. One at a time, briefly dip both sides of about 20 of the ladyfinger cookies in the espresso mixture (don't soak them—it should only take a second or two) and arrange in a single layer in a 13 x 9-inch baking dish. Break the cookies as needed to fit your dish. Spread with half of the mascarpone mixture. Dip and arrange the remaining ladyfingers in another single layer atop the mascarpone mixture, then spread with the remaining mascarpone. Cover and refrigerate until chilled, at least 3 hours.

6. Just before serving, sift the cocoa through a wire sieve over the tiramisù. Using a vegetable peeler, shave chocolate curls from the chocolate bar, letting them fall on top. Cut into squares and serve chilled.

When in Rome . . .

Mascarpone = mass-car-POHN-nay

Joe with his mom and dad. Isn't he the cutest baby?

Vada Via!

It looks so pretty, doesn't it? "Vada via!" Sort of like "Mama Mia," right? It does rhyme, but it means something completely different. *Vada via!* means "get out!" or "go away!" I mean that in the nicest possible way, but now it's time for you to go. My parents are coming over for dinner, Audriana needs a bath, Gia has to write a speech for student council, Gabriella needs to practice her piano, and I'm pretty sure Milania is climbing something somewhere. It's been an honor sharing my kitchen and my family recipes with you. But go, Baby Doll, and rock your family's world with your kick-ass culinary skills. I have no doubt everything you make will be *fabulicious!*

Index